Catholic and Christian

An Explanation of Commonly Misunderstood Catholic Beliefs

Alan Schreck

SERVANT BOOKS
Ann Arbor, Michigan

Copyright © 1984 by Alan Schreck

Book design by John B. Leidy

Cover photo by H. Armstrong Roberts

Available from Servant Publications, Box 8617,
Ann Arbor, Michigan 48107

ISBN 0-89283-181-2
Printed in the United States of America

30   01 02 03 04 05

Nihil obstat: Monsignor Joseph P. Malara
                  Censor Librorum
Imprimatur: † Most Reverend Albert H. Ottenweller
                  Bishop of Steubenville
September 11, 1986
The *nihil obstat* and *imprimatur* are official declarations that a
book or pamphlet is free from doctrinal or moral error. No
implication is contained therein that those *who grant* the *nihil
obstat* or *imprimatur* agree with the contents, opinions, or
statements expressed.

Library of Congress Cataloging in Publication Data

Schreck, Alan.
   Catholic and Christian.

   Includes index.
   1. Catholic Church—Apologetic works.   I. Title.
BX1752.S4 1984   230'.2   84-5412
ISBN 0-89283-181-2 (pbk.)

To Ralph Martin

A prophet in our times whose love of the Lord and zeal for Christian truth has encouraged me and inspired this work.

Acknowledgments

I would like to thank all those who have encouraged and supported me in writing this book. The book is dedicated to Ralph Martin for his inspiration and example to me, and I also thank him for reviewing the manuscript of the book and for providing helpful advice and information.

I would like to acknowledge the on-going support of my colleagues and brothers in the Theology Department at the Franciscan University of Steubenville: Dr. David Ard, Fr. John Bertolucci, Fr. Francis Martin, and especially Fr. Daniel Sinisi, T.O.R.. I would like to thank Nick Cavnar, managing editor of *New Covenant* magazine where some of this material first appeared, for his many contributions to my writing, and also Jim Manney of Servant Publications for his fine editorial work. Thanks are also due to Stephen Patton and Annette Sarcinelli for their assistance in typing.

Finally, I give a special word of appreciation to my wife, Nancy, whose prayers, practical suggestions, typing, and loving support have both enlightened me and lightened the burdens of authorship.

Most of all, thanks and praise are due to God—the source of all wisdom and truth.

Contents

Introduction

A CHRISTIAN IS A PERSON whose primary purpose in life is to know, love, and serve Jesus Christ, the Son of God made man. This common purpose binds all Christians together in a real unity, in spite of our disagreements about specific doctrines.

It is especially important today for Christians to realize that what we have in common—our common Christian beliefs, heritage, and mission—is much greater and more important than whatever divides us. This perspective is crucial today considering the awesome threats and challenges posed to Christianity from the increasingly secularized world, from atheistic philosophies, non-Christian religions, and other ideologies opposed to the gospel of Jesus Christ. (This is not to say that there is no truth or value in the world, other religions, and secular ideologies. However, they are often in open competition with Christianity for the allegiance of men and women.) It seems evident to me that one of the primary strategies of Satan to defeat the gospel and cause of Jesus Christ in the world is to divide Christians—to involve them in arguments among themselves that divert their efforts and attention away from the great commission of Jesus to "make disciples of all the nations" (Mt 28:19)

The purpose of this book is to clarify the Catholic understanding of certain Christian beliefs in order to promote unity among Christians. The title of the book describes how Catholics view themselves: as "Catholic and Christian." Catholics believe that their church and its teachings, while not the only expression of Christianity, *are* genuinely Christian.

Some may ask, "Why is it even necessary to assert this? Isn't

1

it evident that the Catholic Church has been proclaiming that Jesus is Lord for over 1900 years, and has led millions of people to believe in him and follow him?" There are two reasons I see why an explanation of some Catholic teachings is necessary now.

First, many Catholics do not fully understand or live out the Gospel message as officially taught by the Catholic Church. There is confusion and uncertainty among many Catholics about the meaning, the biblical roots, and the practical application of the teachings of their own church.[1]

Secondly, some people today (even committed Christians) are openly stating that the Catholic Church and Catholic doctrine is not Christian, or even "anti-Christian." These allegations are usually based on an incorrect understanding of what the Catholic Church actually teaches.

As a result, Satan has been able to use this lack of understanding (both among Catholics and others) to divide Christians from one another and to divert their attention and energies away from proclaiming the gospel of Jesus Christ and advancing his Kingdom on earth.

Therefore, this book is intended to help Catholics and other concerned Christians to grasp the true meaning of certain commonly misunderstood teachings of the Catholic Church. This analysis should enable Catholics to appreciate and live out their faith more fully and faithfully. It should also help other Christians to approach Catholics as fellow Christians who view their beliefs as rooted in the Bible and supported by the ongoing guidance of the Holy Spirit. I hope that it will be apparent to all that this book was not written to present Catholicism as the only legitimate form of Christianity, and certainly not to critize other Christians, nor to "prove them wrong" in their beliefs.

The first step toward restoring the unity of Christians, which is God's will (Jn 17:21) and so necessary today, is for Christians to understand and respect one another and their beliefs. This does not mean that we will always agree, but it does mean that we will assume that any perceived errors in the life or doctrine of other Christians are honest errors that any good Christian could make.[2]

Even if we do not agree in all points of doctrine, Catholics and other Christians do agree and proclaim together that Jesus Christ is our Lord and Savior, and we are united as Christians in the Holy Spirit, even while we still are divided in our understanding of certain doctrines. My prayer is that this book will contribute to a better understanding of the teaching and tradition of the Catholic Church, so that Catholics and other Christians may grow together in unity in our Christian life and in our common proclamation of the gospel of Jesus Christ.

Prologue:
Perspective on
Catholic Beliefs

A S WE SET OUT to examine what Catholics believe, it is important to begin with an overall perspective on the principles that guide Catholics in recognizing Christian truth. If we understand these principles, we will be better able to understand the specific Catholic beliefs discussed in this book.

These principles and beliefs will appear to be complex and mentally challenging at times. C.S. Lewis, one of my favorite Christian authors, has pointed out, "It is no good asking for a simple religion. After all, real things are not simple. They look simple, but they are not." Lewis says that a wooden table looks simple, but ask a scientist to explain its composition and you encounter a series of "mysteries and complications" that boggle the mind.[1]

Likewise, Christianity, including Catholic Christianity, is not "simple." God has designed it so that a child or the simplest person can understand and accept its basic truths, but a genius can spend a lifetime trying to grasp the full implications of even a single Christian truth. One preacher I know says that the truths of Christianity are so designed that "a mouse can wade in them, but an elephant can swim in them."

I have attempted to keep this presentation of Catholic Christian beliefs as simple as possible, while still unfolding some of its depth and mystery. Let us proceed to consider some of the basic principles which guide the Catholic Church in recognizing Christian truth and in formulating these truths in its doctrinal statements.

Principle I: *God Reveals Christian Truth Through the Holy Spirit*

Where do we go to discover Christian truth? Is it all in the Bible? Catholic Christians believe that the Bible is the inspired word of God, and a "norm" for judging the truth of all Christian beliefs. That is, no Christian belief can outrightly contradict the teaching of the Bible. The Second Letter to Timothy declares: "All scripture is inspired of God and is useful for teaching—for reproof, correction, and training in holiness so that the man of God may be fully competent and equipped for every good work" (2 Tm 3:16-17). Catholics believe that this teaching applies to all scripture—both the Hebrew scripture or "Old Testament," and the Christian scripture, the "New Testament."

"All scripture is inspired of God..." But does this mean that *only* scripture is inspired? Catholics do not find this teaching in the Bible. While Catholics believe that the Bible is the foremost and unsurpassed source of God's revelation, they also believe that God reveals his truth and guides his people in other ways. For example, the New Testament records that the Holy Spirit revealed God's truth through the gift of prophecy (Acts 11:27-30; 21:10-12; 1 Cor 14:1-4, 31), councils of church leaders (Acts 15:28), and even direct revelations to individuals, such as to Peter (Acts 10:9-17) and Paul (Acts 9, 18:9, 20:22-23, 27:24). Certainly these manifestations of the Holy Spirit had to be "tested" or discerned—an important responsibility of the church's leaders. Even the writings that now comprise the New Testament had to be discerned by those same church leaders before they were accepted as the inspired word of God.

Catholics believe that the revelation of God in the Bible is one important way that God reveals himself and guides his people. But the Holy Spirit has also been sent by Jesus to be the church's continual guide. The Spirit expands and deepens the church's understanding of God's truth and will over the course of history. The Bible is a primary work of God's revelation to mankind, but not the only work. The Second Vatican Council taught that Catholics should not think that there are two sources of revelation, the Bible and "tradition," but that there is actually only *one* word of God that has been revealed and passed on in written form (the Bible), and also in other forms, such as preaching, spiritual gifts, the church's worship, and other unwritten forms inspired or guided by the Holy Spirit.

In other words, Catholics believe that the Bible is the "book of Christianity," but not that Christianity is a "religion of the book" like Judaism. Christianity is not a religion of the written word alone, but of the Holy Spirit. Later we will discuss more fully how the Holy Spirit is present among God's people to guide them and reveal God's truth.

Principle II: The Incarnational Principle

Catholics believe that the Incarnation, God becoming man in Jesus Christ, reveals an important truth about the way God chooses to relate to mankind. God could have continued to reveal himself to the human race solely through visions, voices, or angelic messengers. Instead he chose to "empty himself" (Phil 2:7) and stoop down to our level by becoming a true man—a man that humans could see, hear, and touch. Jesus himself used ordinary physical objects, human gestures, and even other people to reveal God's presence and love. He used water, bread, wine, fish, his touch, and even mud made with his spit, to manifest the love and power of the Father working through him. He gave his apostles, who were ordinary men, the same power and authority that he had to heal, expel demons, and to use the same signs that he used (water, bread, wine, touch, etc.) to make the presence and power of God visible.

Why? Why did God himself take on humanity? Why did Jesus choose ordinary men and use ordinary objects and gestures to show forth and transmit the power of God? Why? Because God knows what human beings are like, and what they need. God created man as an earthly, physical creature who experiences reality through his body and his five senses, and not just through his "spirit." Man is an *embodied* spirit, and God stoops down to our level because he knows that we need to relate to him through what is physical, visible, and tangible. Yes, God also calls mankind to have faith and hope in things that are unseen, which are eternal (2 Cor 4:18). But he graciously uses the things we can see, feel, hear, and touch to reveal his presence and love, and even to give himself to us and share his life with us fully.

What are the practical implications of this principle? Catholics believe that since the Incarnation, God has continued to relate to mankind (revealing his love and giving his life to us) in a human way—using physical objects, human gestures, and men and women whom he has set apart to be his representatives through the commission of Jesus Christ. Catholics believe that God intended there to be effective, visible signs of God's presence and power, which Catholics call "sacraments." These are physical things such as water, oil, salt, bread, and wine, which make visible God's presence, power, and blessing. Catholics also believe that God can use pictures, statues, medals, and other objects to remind us of him, and of his work in holy men and women whom he has raised up for us to imitate. Catholics believe that God uses certain human beings to continue the ministry of Jesus in the world, as successors of his original apostles. All these things are related to the "incarnational" principle. This principle affirms that the church, like Jesus, is not only a spiritual reality, but also a human and earthly one. There is nothing human or of the earth that God cannot and does not use to reveal and communicate his love for us. (St. Francis of Assisi, the patron of the University where I teach, is one of the great men of God who most appreciated this truth and expressed it in his life and teaching.) Hence Catholics believe that we are called to recognize that God uses the material, physical, and human dimension of life to direct our attention and love to him and to his work. Since "the Word became flesh" (Jn 1:14) as Jesus Christ, the whole human perspective on the value of this world and the true purpose of the things of the world has been entirely transformed.

Principle III: The Hierarchy of Truths

Catholics believe that God reveals the fullness of truth to Christians through the Bible and through the ongoing guidance of the Holy Spirit. There are a wide range of truths that Catholics believe are revealed by God. Some of these truths are accepted by nearly all Christians, such as the divinity of Jesus, the Trinity, Jesus' intention to establish a church, and many others. Other truths are accepted by Catholics, but not by other Christians, such as the importance of Mary in God's plan of salvation, the intercessory role of the saints, the existence of purgatory, and so on. Catholics believe that both the former and the latter categories are part of the fullness of Christian truth. So, Catholics do not distinguish between "Christian truths" and "Catholic truths," as if Catholic beliefs were something added on to "basic Christianity." Rather, Catholics understand the official teachings of the Catholic Church to be a faithful presentation of the fullness of divine truth that God has revealed through the Bible and the ongoing revelation of the Holy Spirit.

However, having said this, an important qualification needs to be made in order to understand Catholic teaching correctly. Catholics do not believe that all revealed truths are equally central to the basic gospel message or are equally important for salvation. This is what the Catholic Church means when it teaches that there is a "hierarchy of truths." The Second Vatican Council taught that when Catholics and other Christians meet to compare doctrines, "they should remember that in Catholic teaching there exists an order or 'hierarchy' of truths, since they [these truths] vary in their relationship to the foundation of Christian faith."[2]

Practically speaking, this means that the beliefs that are most important for Catholics are truths such as the divinity of Jesus, the necessity of his death on the cross for our salvation, the reality and power of the Holy Spirit, and so on.[3] Here Catholics find a common ground of understanding and cooperation with other Christians, because Catholics and most other Christians usually agree on the most central and basic doctrines of Christianity. However, Catholics believe that there are other Christian truths, such as those concerning Mary, the saints, purgatory, and so on, that are indeed true, but are not the central points of the Gospel message. It is important for both Catholics and other Christians to recognize this distinction. Sometimes Catholics are guilty of viewing and talking about Mary, the saints, purgatory, and similar beliefs as if they were the most important Christian truths. This often produces an unnecessary obstacle to unity with other Christians, and may actually be a distortion of authentic Christianity. On the other hand, sometimes other Christians focus unduly on Catholic beliefs about Mary, the saints, purgatory, indulgences, and the like (often rejecting them in a one-sided way, even when they have some basis in the Bible) in order to portray Catholics as "un-Christian", or to accuse the Catholic church of distorting the Gospel of Jesus Christ. These extremes should be avoided, and corrected where they exist.

Catholic Christians want to be faithful to the full gospel and to the guidance of the Holy Spirit. If the Bible and the experience of Christians over the course of centuries testify to certain truths about Mary, the saints, the next life, certain ways of prayer and worship, and so on, Catholics want to acknowledge and embrace these truths, even if they are less central in the "hierarchy" of Christian truths. Rather than rejecting these truths as non-essential, Catholic Christians try to retain them but keep them in the proper perspective, not exaggerating them or focusing on them unduly. Catholics admit that, in practice, they have not always kept the proper balance in their beliefs. They have not always lived out the fullness of Christian truth that the Catholic Church professes to preserve and proclaim in its official doctrine. This is why Catholics admit their need and desire for ongoing repentance and renewal.

Catholics understand that God has gifted his church with a rich storehouse of truths, all of which have a place in God's plan and in the Christian life. Catholics do not wish to impoverish the richness or fullness of truth by rejecting or neglecting any truths, even if they are not basic or central to Christianity. Rather, Catholics seek the Holy Spirit's wisdom and help in order to hold to *all* the truths of Christianity, and to keep them in the proper perspective and balance, both in belief and practice. As leading Catholic ecumenist, Kilian McDonnell, O.S.B., has written in an article concerning Mary and Christian unity:

> Though the term "full gospel" is strange to Roman Catholic ears, it represents a principle with which Catholics are at home: the proclamation of the full plan of salvation. When Roman Catholics neglect aspects of that full gospel they welcome the corrective witness of classical Pentecostals and others. Indeed the historical churches, Catholic and Protestant, owe a debt to classical Pentecostals for witnessing to the role of the Spirit and his gifts. On the other hand, neither Roman Catholics . . . nor classical Pentecostals, nor others should violate the principle of the full gospel by neglecting those passages of the New Testament which mention Mary [for example]. No zones of

silence should be established on the unspoken assumption that passages mentioning Mary [or any other Christian truth] should be omitted when proclaiming the full gospel.[4]

Catholic Christians want to believe in, proclaim, and live the "full gospel," even though it is a challenge to keep all the truths revealed by God in the proper order, perspective, or "hierarchy." Individual Catholics must not think that they can "pick and choose" among Christian truths, only believing those that they find personally acceptable. The truths that the Catholic Church teaches have been discussed, discerned, tested, and finally handed on over the course of centuries. This discernment process involved careful reflection on the Bible and the guidance of the Holy Spirit working through the church and its leaders. These truths were not arrived at easily, or concocted overnight.

A Catholic pastor I heard recently compared the fullness of Christian truth to a Christmas gift that did not come fully completed (Jn 16:12-14), but that required assembly over time using all the parts provided. In the assembly of such a gift, you need to use all the parts. If you only use fifty parts out of eighty, the gift will never operate—at least not in the way the manufacturer intended! Catholics believe that Christian truth is a gift of God like that. It has many parts or aspects and we are not in a position to omit certain parts and include others. We also must follow the "instructions," the guidance of the Holy Spirit Jesus promised to the church, to insure that all the parts (all aspects of Christian truth) fit together in the right way. Catholics believe that the Holy Spirit has been given to the church to guide God's people into all aspects of Christian truth, and to bring forth this truth according to God's order and perspective.

Let us now proceed to examine these aspects of Christian truth, as Catholic Christians understand them.

ONE

Salvation: God's Free Gift in Jesus Christ

CHRISTIANITY IS GOD'S REVELATION about himself and his relationship to mankind. This book will begin by focusing on some basic truths about God, creation, the fall of man from God's friendship, and God's plan to redeem the human race through Jesus Christ. As we review these truths, please remember that this book is not a catechism. It does not provide a full presentation of the Catholic faith, but rather emphasizes aspects of Catholic belief that are often misunderstood—by both Catholics and others. You will find this emphasis throughout the whole book. Most of what I say here is accepted by all Christians. But I will frequently single out and discuss questions that are in some way controversial. They are sources of misunderstanding between Catholics and Protestants and are even more difficult to deal with when the genuine teachings of the churches are misrepresented or understood imperfectly. Consequently, I take up these questions out of a conviction that a genuine commitment to Christian unity demands that such issues be faced squarely in order that misunderstandings on both sides of the dialogue be resolved and so that the Lord may draw Christians together in a unity based on his truth.

Some Basic Truths About Salvation

Three Persons in One God. The central belief of the Catholic Church is that God is one in three persons— Father, Son, and Holy Spirit. These three persons are distinct, but equal in power, majesty, and divinity. The "Trinity" is the name that the early Christians gave to the one God comprised of three equal and distinct divine persons.

God Alone Is to Be Worshipped. Catholic Christians believe that the one God *alone*—the Father, Son, and Holy Spirit—is to be worshipped and adored. The first commandment of the law of Moses still holds true for Christians: "I am the Lord your God.... You shall have no other gods before me" (Ex 20:2, 3; Dt 5:6, 7). Jesus taught, "You shall love the Lord your God with all your heart, and with all your soul, and with all your mind. This is the great and first commandment." (Mt 22:37, 38)

Catholics may honor or venerate God's creatures, but worship is reserved for God alone. The prayers of Catholics are ultimately directed to the one God. Catholics may honor other exemplary Christians of the past or present, and even ask them to pray for us, but the prayers of all God's people finally are directed only to God. All official prayers of the Catholic Church, such as the Mass, are prayers finally directed "to the Father, through the Son, and in the Holy Spirit."

God the Creator and Savior. Catholics believe that God created everything out of nothing. The Nicene Creed proclaims, "We believe in one God, the Father almighty, creator of heaven and earth, of all that is seen or unseen."

Why did God create? Simply to express his overflowing goodness and love. The Book of Genesis affirms that all God created was good—very good. As the "crown" or climax of his creation, God created man, male and female, in his "image and likeness." This means that man reflected God's goodness, his wisdom, his power to love, and his dominion over creation.

Man also shared in God's power to choose freely and to direct his own path in life. The Book of Genesis reveals that it was man's abuse of his power to choose freely that disrupted his harmonious, intimate relationship with God. Man used his free will to disobey God because he was deceived by Satan (a fallen rebellious angel, the arch-foe of God) disguised as a serpent.[1] This first rebellion of man against God, which Catholics call "original sin," disrupted man's intimate, loving relationship with his creator, and introduced a seemingly permanent and irreparable rift between God and mankind. Henceforth, every human being on earth would be born into this fallen condition, this state of separation or alienation from God, which is called "original sin." As the apostle Paul wrote: "...through one man sin entered the world and with sin, death, death thus coming to all men inasmuch as all sinned..." (Rom 5:12).[2]

Human beings can do nothing to reverse the effects of man's first rebellion against God, and to restore man's loving relationship with his Creator. But what is impossible for man is possible for God. A ray of hope for mankind appeared as soon as the fall occurred. in Genesis 3:15, immediately after the account of the fall of man, God told Satan that from the "seed" or descendants of the woman he had deceived would come one who would "bruise" or "strike at" his head. Catholics view this as the first foreshadowing or prophecy of the coming of a savior for mankind.

The Old Testament recounts the unfolding of God's plan to heal and restore mankind's relationship with him. It foretells a savior, or messiah, who will bring about this restoration. Many of God's people of the Old Covenant (the Jewish people) interpreted these Old Testament prophecies in political terms, expecting the savior or messiah to be a great king, like David, who would save them once-for-all from all political oppression and establish a lasting, unshakable kingdom for God's people in this world.

Jesus—The True Messiah and Savior. When Jesus of Nazareth began his public ministry, he stirred the deep-seated hopes and longings of his Jewish hearers with the message: "The time is fulfilled, and the Kingdom of God is at hand; repent, and believe in the gospel!" (Mk 1:15). Was this the Messiah who had finally come to establish the reign of God on earth? Christians answer "Yes!" As his ministry unfolded, Jesus made it clear that his mission and the kingdom he proclaimed was not political. It was far bigger than that. He came to overcome man's separation from God, and restore both man's first rebellion (original sin) and every sin which followed. He came to reverse all of the effects of sin: man's suffering, sicknesses, and even man's greatest enemy, death. He came to subdue and conquer all spiritual powers and forces opposed to God, including God's archenemy, Satan. God's plan would not be completed until all things, "things in heaven and things on earth," were united in Jesus Christ and "put under his feet (dominion)" (Eph 1:10, 22). Jesus' mission had eternal, cosmic dimensions.

Jesus As Fully God and Fully Man. Who could accomplish such a mission? A mere man? By no means. Only God himself has the power to restore man and all creation to right order and a right relationship to himself. Christians believe that Jesus of Nazareth, a genuine, full human being (Heb 2:14, 17), is also truly and fully God. Jesus revealed himself to be the "only-begotten" Son of God the Father, fully equal to the Father in eternity, power, and glory. John's Gospel calls him the eternal Word of God, who "became flesh" and "dwelt among us" as Jesus Christ (Jn 1:1-14). Later Christians explained that Jesus Christ is the "second person of the Trinity" made man—God incarnate. Christians believe and proclaim that God the Son became man to restore mankind and all creation to union with God. Man's initial destiny in God's plan, to live forever in perfect joy with God, is once again made possible by Jesus Christ.

> For God so loved the world that he gave his only Son, that whoever believes in him should not perish but have eternal life. For God sent the Son into the world, not to condemn the world, but that the world might be saved through him.
>
> (Jn 3:16-17)

How Catholic Christians Understand Salvation

The Good News: Salvation in Jesus Christ. The ultimate meaning of "salvation" for human beings is that we "should not perish, but have eternal life." We are saved *from* sin, from the condition of rebellion and separation from God that finally results in eternal death, and saved *for* eternal life and happiness with God.

The Catholic Church has always affirmed that salvation is a gift that God freely offers to mankind. God "desires all men to be saved and to come to the knowledge of the truth" (1 Tm 2:4). God is "the Savior of all men, especially of those who believe" (1 Tm 4:10). Human beings cannot save themselves. Nor does mankind "deserve" eternal life, any more than we "deserved" to be created in the first place. Nothing that a person has ever done or ever could do *on his own* can "merit" or "earn" eternal life; God must offer it and confer it.

The Good News is that God has offered this free gift of salvation to mankind. How does this salvation come to us? How does God offer it? First of all, the Catholic Church teaches that salvation comes only through Jesus Christ. "And there is salvation in no one else, for there is no other name under heaven given among men by which we must be saved" (Acts 4:12). The Catholic Church also teaches that Jesus saved us through his passion and death on the cross (Gal 6:14; Col 1:20, 2:14; 1 Cor 2:2), and that the blood of Christ shed for the salvation of the world brings a saving and healing power (Rom 3:25; Heb 9;13, 14; 1 Pt 1:2, 18-19; 1 Jn 1:7; Rv 1:5, 5:9, 7:14, 12:11).

How central is this to the faith of Catholic Christians? Take note that the central religious symbol for Catholics— found everywhere in Catholic churches, schools, and hospitals—is the *crucifix*, the image of Jesus Christ dying on the cross and shedding his blood for our salvation.

Is There Salvation Outside of Jesus Christ?

The Catholic Church does not teach and has never taught that a person may be "saved" (reconciled to God and brought to eternal life with him) by anyone other than Jesus Christ. No one is saved by Buddha, Mohammed, or the leaders or gods of any other religions. Nor, I might add, do Catholics believe that anyone is saved by the Pope, Mary, the saints, or any other member of the church. Jesus alone is the savior of man: "… there is salvation in no one else for there is no other name under heaven given among men by which we must be saved" (Acts 4:12).

Recent official teachings of the Catholic Church illustrate this insistence that Jesus is the only way to salvation:

For Christ, made present to us in His Body, which is the Church, is the one Mediator and the unique Way of salvation.[3]

… as the Church has always held and continues to hold, Christ in His boundless love freely underwent His passion and death because of the sins of all men, so that all might attain salvation. It is, therefore, the duty of the Church's preaching to proclaim the cross of Christ as the sign of God's all-embracing love and as the fountain from which every grace flows.[4]

The specific purpose of this [the Church's] missionary activity is evangelization and the planting of the Church among those peoples and groups where she has not yet taken root.... The chief means of this implantation is the preaching of the gospel of Jesus Christ.... This missionary activity finds its reason in the will of God, "who wishes all men to be saved and come to the knowledge of the truth. For there is one God, and one Mediator between God and men, himself man, Christ Jesus who gave himself as a ransom for all" (1 Tm 2:4-5), "neither is there salvation in any other" (Acts 4:12).

Therefore, all must be converted to Him as he is made known by the Church's preaching....[5]

For further study on what the Catholic Church teaches on this subject, I recommend Pope John Paul II's first encyclical letter, *The Redeemer of Man (Redemptor Hominis)*. The letter begins: "The Redeemer of man, Jesus Christ, is the center of the universe and history." Also examine the documents of the Second Vatican Council. The council's opening message, addressed to all mankind, proclaimed:

We believe that the Father so loved the world that He gave His own Son to save it. Indeed, through this same Son of His He freed us from bondage to sin, reconciling all things unto Himself through Him, "making peace through the blood of his cross" [Col 1:20], so that "we might be called sons of God and truly be such."[6]

In short, a thorough study of the official statements of Popes and councils of bishops through the last 19 centuries will affirm that the basic *kerygma* (proclamation) of the Catholic Church has always been the same as that of Peter on the day of Pentecost: "Let all the house of Israel know assuredly that God has made him both Lord and Christ, this Jesus whom you crucified" (Acts 2:36). What about the salvation of those who have not yet committed themselves to Jesus Christ? The Catholic Church makes no firm judgment about their salvation, but leaves open the possibility that God may save some persons who, through no fault of their own, have not accepted the gospel of Jesus Christ. The last judgment scene in Mt 25:31-46 speaks of the judgment of "the nations" on the basis of works of charity; belief in Jesus Christ is not mentioned. Romans 2:12-16 says that "gentiles without the law" will be judged according to God's law "written in their hearts" or "conscience." These appear to be exceptional cases, however. The Second Vatican Council insisted that

> ... though God in ways known to Himself can lead those inculpably ignorant of the gospel to that faith without which it is impossible to please him (Heb 11:6), yet a necessity lies upon the Church (cf. 1 Cor 9:16), and at the same time a sacred duty, to preach the gospel. Hence, missionary activity today as always retains its power and necessity.[7]

Thus, Catholic Christians must avoid two extremes in considering the salvation of non-Christians. They should avoid presuming that those who don't believe in Jesus and his gospel will necessarily be condemned, but neither should Catholics presume that these people will be saved without accepting the gospel. What the Second Vatican Council taught unambiguously is that man's salvation comes only through the death and resurrection of Jesus Christ, and that it is the church's mission and solemn duty to proclaim this "good news" to all people.

Receiving God's Gift of Salvation

Catholics believe that salvation is a free gift, flowing from the grace (or "graciousness") of God. "For by grace you have been saved, through faith: and this is not your own doing, it is the gift of God" (Eph 2:8).

A gift, however, can either be accepted or refused. This is also true of the gift of salvation. Catholics believe that while God *offers* all men the grace to believe in him and do good (see 1 Tm 2:4), each person must freely choose to accept that gift. Being made in God's "image and likeness" means that we have a genuinely free will—the power to accept God's saving grace, or to reject it. This free will has been weakened by sin, but not destroyed; it is influenced by social and psychological forces, but not totally controlled by them. The Bible indicates that man has free will by the fact that Jesus and all the authors of scripture constantly exhort and challenge people to repent (literally in the Greek, "to change your mind"), to believe, and to do good. The gospel message implies that *anyone,* by the grace God freely offers to all, can make a decision to change and become a follower of Jesus Christ. Some people who hear the gospel repent and believe; others don't. Catholics believe that this happens because God has given every person the ability to make a real choice to accept or reject the grace he freely offers.

How does a person receive God's gift of salvation? The Bible mentions a number of aspects that are part of our response to God's gift. Catholics try to consider all of these aspects in order to make the fullest possible response to God's word. Taken together, these elements of our response, found in scripture, give a complete answer to the question, "What must I do to be saved?"

What Is Faith? Jesus' first recorded command was "Repent, and believe in the gospel" (Mk 1:15) and the New Testament clearly states that salvation is received by faith in God through Jesus Christ. Catholics firmly believe in the importance of faith in accepting God's gift of salvation. "I solemnly assure you," Jesus said, "the man who hears my word and has faith in him who sent me possesses eternal life" (Jn 5:24). Many other New Testament texts affirm that faith in Jesus Christ leads to salvation. (See Mk

16:16; Jn 3:16, 6:28-29, 11:25-27, 20:30-31; Eph 2:8-10; 2 Thes 2:13.)

What is faith? The New Testament shows faith to be much more than an intellectual assent to the proposition that God exists or that Jesus Christ is Lord and Savior. This assent may be a first step, but it is not sufficient for salvation. Even evil spirits recognize and acknowledge Jesus' true identity. An unclean spirit cried out: "I know who you are, the Holy One of God" (Mk 1:24). James declared, "Even the demons believe—and shudder" (Jas 2:19).

The faith that leads to salvation is an act of acknowledging our utter dependence on God and committing our lives totally to Him. When Jesus spoke about faith, proclaiming, "believe in God, believe also in me" (Jn 14:1), he meant, "give your whole life to me; follow me; obey me; become my disciple." True Christian faith means entrusting your whole life to God. it is a commitment to put God first and to do whatever he commands or asks. As the Second Vatican Council explained:

> By faith, man freely commits his entire self to God, making the full submission of his intellect and will to God....[8]

The Catholic Church today emphasizes the pre-eminence of faith in its official teaching. The "Decree on the Apostolate of the Laity" sums up this teaching well:

> The Church's mission is concerned with the salvation of men; and men win salvation through the grace of Christ and faith in him.[9]

Many Christians today equate "faith" with a "decision for Christ"—a conscious, personal acceptance of Jesus Christ as the Lord and Savior of your life. This terminology is used mostly by evangelical Protestants, but Catholics agree that all mature Christians must make a conscious choice to accept Jesus Christ as their Lord and Savior and to commit themselves to follow him. Catholics make such a public recommitment every year when they renew their baptismal promises during the Easter liturgy. The practice of regular, even daily, personal "acts of faith" in Jesus Christ is a part of Catholic tradition.

Unfortunately, some Catholics have neglected the importance of this conscious, personal commitment to Jesus Christ. Catholics sometimes assume that persons who are baptized, attend Mass, and receive the sacraments regularly have obviously accepted Jesus Christ as the Lord and Savior of their lives. Pastoral experience with U.S. Catholics shows that this is often not the case; many Catholics have not yet made a deliberate, adult decision to believe in Jesus Christ and give their lives fully to him. In response to this, the Catholic Church has placed a strong emphasis in recent years on evangelization (even of the baptized), on continual conversion to Christ, and on spiritual renewal. The goal of all of these is to lead all Catholics (and eventually all people) to a full personal faith in Jesus Christ.

It is also part of Catholic teaching to consider "faith" as a *way of life* rather than as a major decision that happens once, twice, or a few times in one's life. Catholics realize the importance of the initial conversion and commitment to Christ, but they also emphasize the challenge of living out faith in Jesus Christ every day, by God's grace and with the guidance of the Holy Spirit. God provides the power (or grace) to live out our faith through many channels: through daily prayer, the sacraments, and our life and fellowship with other Christians. Thus, these means of God's grace are also significant for our salvation, since they enable us to persevere in our faith and live it out day by day. Later in this chapter we will consider two of these "channels" of God's grace: the sacraments and the church.

Even though many things play a part in receiving God's gift of salvation, faith is primary, for two reasons. First, a Christian's good works flow from a firm belief and trust in God. Secondly, receiving the sacraments, observing church teaching, and using the other means of grace are meaningless without a living faith in God.

At the same time, salvation is a process that depends entirely on God. None of the individual elements or means of salvation that are discussed in this chapter have any magical power to save us. We can do many good works and yet be alienated from God and resist his grace. We can be baptized without living our baptismal promises. We can go to Mass on Sunday and sin the rest of the week. Even faith is a gift of God, not something we earn. Faith cannot save us if we deny that faith by the way we live. Again, as James said, "even the demons believe—and shudder" (Jas 2:19).

Faith and Good Works

Catholics believe that the life of faith is also a life of charity or "good works." This life of faith is a life of love of God and neighbor that expresses itself in one's thoughts, attitudes, speech, and actions. Therefore let us examine the relationship between a Christian's faith and good works, and their importance for salvation.

Catholics do not sharply separate "faith" and "good works" or charity. By "good works" Catholics do not mean the "works of the law" that Paul condemns, but rather the "works" of active charity or love that flow from living faith in Jesus Christ. Those who follow God will do whatever God commands or asks of them, and their "works" truly will reflect their faith. This is the point that James was making in his letter:

My brothers, what good is it to profess faith without practicing it? Such faith has no power to save one, has it? If a brother or sister has nothing to wear and no food for the day, and you say to them, "Goodbye and good luck! Keep warm and well fed; but do not meet their bodily needs, what good is that? So it is with the faith that does nothing in practice. It is thoroughly lifeless. (Jas 2:14-18)

In other words, Catholics believe that true faith will express itself in a person's "works"—the way the person actually lives. Is this understanding biblical? Jesus and the New Testament authors insist that people will be judged not only by their faith, but according to their actual conduct or works. Jesus warned, "not everyone who says to me, 'Lord, Lord.' will enter the kingdom of heaven, but only he who does the will of my Father in heaven" (Mt 7:21). A number of other passages speak of the role of good works in salvation (see Mt 16:27; Rom 2:5-10; 2 Cor 5:10; Jas 2:14-26; 1 Pt 1:17).

Even the apostle Paul, who strongly corrects those who try to justify themselves before God by performing "works of the law" (strictly observing all the Jewish traditions), also states: "...[God] will render to every man according to his works" (Rom 2:6), and "we must all appear before the judgment seat of Christ, so that each one may receive good or evil according to what he has done in the body" (2 Cor 5:10).

In summary, when the Catholic Church speaks of Good works as a "means of salvation," it is expressing a belief found in the Bible: Genuine faith requires an active response, which is charity, love, or good works. Paul called this "faith working through love" (Gal 5:6, RSV), or "faith, which expresses itself through love" (Gal 5:6, NAB).

The Catholic teaching about the role of faith and "works" in man's salvation has often been misunderstood—by both Catholics and Protestants. Although it remains a source of division between Catholics and Protestants even today, many Protestants and Catholics may be surprised to learn what the Catholic Church actually teaches about this.

After the Reformation, the Roman Catholic bishops clarified their teaching on justification and salvation in the

"Decree on Justification" issued at the Council of Trent in 1547. This decree affirmed, first, that salvation and justification, two terms closely related in the New Testament, are free gifts or graces of God that come only from Jesus Christ.[10] This grace or gift of justification comes before either faith or good works, since faith and works are only ways by which we accept God's free gift or grace of salvation. As Trent stated this, we are "said to be justified gratuitously (i.e., by grace), because none of those things which precede justification, whether faith or works, merit the grace itself of justification, for 'if it is a grace, it is not now by reason of works, otherwise (as the same Apostle says) grace would no longer be grace' [Rom 11:6]."[11] The first point, then, is that justification and salvation are free gifts or graces of God that are not earned by any work of man, even faith.

Secondly, the Council of Trent affirmed that the first and most important way to receive God's gift of salvation or justification is through faith. The Catholic bishops declared:

> We are therefore said to be justified by faith, because "faith is the beginning of human salvation," the foundation and root of all justification; "without which it is impossible to please God"(Heb 11:6) and to enter the fellowship of his sons.[12]

Thirdly, the Council of Trent also noted that the Bible exhorts those who are justified by God's grace to keep the commandments, to perform good works, and to be prepared to suffer as Christ suffered. (e.g., 1 Cor 15:58). "... always abound(ing) in the work of the Lord, knowing that in the Lord your labor is not in vain"; Heb 6:10, "for God is not so unjust as to overlook your work and the love which you showed for His sake..." Nonetheless, the Council of Trent insisted that

... although in the sacred Writings so much is ascribed to good works that even "he that shall give a drink of cold water to one of his least ones," Christ promises, "shall not lose his reward" (Mt 10:42)... ; nevertheless far be it that a Christian should either trust or "glory" in himself and not "in the Lord" [cf. 1 Cor 1:31; 2 Cor 10:17), whose goodness towards all men is so great that He wishes the things that are His gifts to be their own merits.[13]

The Sacraments and Salvation

Catholics believe that the sacraments are channels by which the grace of Jesus Christ comes to us. They too are part of God's plan of salvation. Let us consider the significance for salvation of the two primary sacraments: baptism and the Eucharist (or the Lord's Supper).

The Bible attests that baptism is the way a person becomes part of the body of Christ, the church. At the end of his speech on Pentecost, Peter told his hearers what they had to do to be saved: "Repent and be baptized everyone of you in the name of Jesus Christ for the forgiveness of your sins, and you shall receive the gift of the Holy Spirit" (Acts 2:38). Through baptism, converts to Jesus Christ first received forgiveness of their sins, the gift of the Holy Spirit, and became members of the community of Christians, the church. But does baptism have anything to do with salvation? Jesus said, "He who believes and is baptized will be saved" (Mk 16:16). He told Nicodemus that "unless one is born of water and the Spirit, he cannot enter the kingdom of God" (Jn 3:5). The church of New Testament times responded to this teaching by immediately baptizing all new converts (see Acts 2:38, 41; 18:8; 19:5; 22:16). Paul explained that baptism unites believers to Jesus in his death so that they will also share in his resurrection (Rom 6:3-5). Baptism, then, is also a means to salvation.

Does the Eucharist or Lord's Supper have any significance for salvation? Jesus told the Jews:

> Unless you eat the flesh of the Son of Man and drink his blood, you have no life in you; he who eats my flesh and drinks my blood has eternal life, and I will raise him up at the last day. (Jn 6:53-54)

The apostle Paul explained that eating the flesh of Christ and drinking his blood refers to partaking of the bread and cup of the Eucharist (1 Cor 10:16), which Jesus commanded his disciples to do in his memory (Lk 22:19; 1 Cor 11:23-26). The sacraments and their role in God's saving plan will be discussed more fully in Chapter Seven.

The Church and Salvation

The Catholic understanding of the church will also be discussed fully later, but here we will examine the importance of the church for salvation. In its broadest definition, the church is the community or body of persons committed to following Jesus Christ. Catholic Christians believe that the normal way to be saved is to become a follower of Jesus, and thus to become part of "the church which is his [Christ's] body" (Eph 1:22-23).

For centuries, Christians accepted the teaching of St. Cyprian of Carthage, a great bishop-martyr of the third century, who said, "Outside of the church there is no salvation."[14] Cyprian's teaching was based on certain presuppositions that were shared by the authors of the New Testament. They presupposed that one was saved by becoming a follower of Jesus, and that followers of Jesus were members of his body, the church. They also presupposed that the church's members would respect and obey their leaders, because Jesus Christ had given them authority to guide God's people.

All this seemed self-evident to the early Christians. There was no salvation outside the church because it was only within the church that a person had access to the ways by which he could come into contact with Jesus, and thus be saved. (See Acts 2 and 4.)

Therefore, Catholics believe that the church itself is an important means of salvation. Jesus himself indicated this when he told Peter that "the gates of Sheol will not prevail against it [the church]" (Mt 16:18).

This does not mean that Catholics believe that a person must belong to the Catholic Church to be saved. In fact, as recently as 1949, the Roman Catholic Church vigorously rejected an opinion, attributed to Fr. Leonard Feeney of Boston, that only Catholics could be saved. (Fr. Feeney later clarified his views which were then found to be in accordance with Catholic teaching.)

St. Augustine, in *The City of God,* said that some persons would be saved who truly love God, even if they were not formally members of the (Catholic) Church. On the other hand, Augustine warned his fellow Catholics that some baptized members of the church would not be saved if they did not love God and live in charity.[15] Church membership may be a great help to an individual in attaining salvation, but it is never an automatic "ticket to heaven."

The Catholic Church's official teaching is very similar to Augustine's. The Second Vatican Council, after spelling out what it means to be a "fully incorporated" member of the church, insisted:

> He is not saved, however, who, though he is part of the body of the Church, does not persevere in charity. He remains indeed in the bosom of the Church, but, as it were, only in a "bodily" manner, and not "in his heart." All the sons of the Church should remember that their exalted status is to be attributed not to their own merits but to the special grace of Christ. If they fail moreover to respond to that grace in thought, word, and deed, not

only will they not be saved but they will be the more severely judged.[16]

This is a stern warning to "nominal Catholics." They will not escape rigorous judgment by God on the last day simply because they are Catholics.

Church Law and Salvation

How important, then, do Catholics consider obedience to specific teachings or disciplines of their church for salvation? Catholics and non-Catholics alike wonder whether Catholics believe that they will lose their salvation for missing Mass on Sunday, refusing to fast on a specific fast day, or rejecting an officially defined Catholic doctrine, such as the Immaculate Conception of Mary.

To answer this question adequately, it must be seen in a broader context of Catholic Christian belief. Catholics believe that Jesus gave his apostles authority to govern and guide the church, and that this authority was passed on by the apostles to the elders who came after them. As we will discuss in detail later, the bishops were the primary elders who carried on the mission of the apostles and exercised their authority in the church in the name of Jesus Christ. The bishops understood the words of Jesus to his apostles to apply to themselves as well: "He who hears you, hears me, and he who rejects you, rejects me" (Lk 10:16). The early Christians believed that the bishops' authority was from God, just as they accepted that the authority of the apostles as a gift of the Holy Spirit.

Catholics today still believe that the authority of the bishops and the pope is God's authority, given to them by Jesus himself through the apostles and their successors down through the ages. Therefore, a Catholic who obstinately rejects the official teachings or directives of the bishops (or the "chief bishop," the pope) might be guilty of a form of rebellion against God which would jeopardize the person's salvation. In the early church, those who rejected the bishops' teaching were expelled from the community. This "excommunication" was a public pronouncement that the person was no longer in communion or unity with the church because they were not in submission to the recognized elders and their teaching. Excommunication does not necessarily mean that a person will not be saved. The point, however, is that the rebellion against the church's teaching that brings about excommunication could very well indicate a deeper rebellion against God's plan and his authority.

This understanding of the authority of the bishops to govern the church presupposes a basic trust that the Holy Spirit truly guides and inspires them in their leadership. The bishops could not teach or require anything that directly contradicts the word of God in the Bible, because one of their primary duties is to teach and defend the word of God, and to interpret it faithfully under the guidance of the Holy Spirit.

But what about when people taking a serious look at the Catholic faith—whether they be Catholics from birth or others investigating Catholicism—find themselves struggling to accept some official Catholic teaching? It may be a challenging theological doctrine such as the mystery of Mary's immaculate conception, or a moral teaching such as the Catholic Church's rejection of artificial contraception as a means of birth regulation. The Catholic Church recognizes that persons seeking to form their views and consciences through the teachings of the Bible and the Church may find themselves temporarily struggling to understand and assent to a particular teaching. In such cases, one's salvation would not be jeopardized. However, a Catholic who is earnestly seeking to follow the Lord will invariably come to recognize the purpose and wisdom of church teachings and discipline, or at least be willing to accept the church's

judgment in faith and trust, even if they do not fully understand it or agree with it. They trust that Jesus promised to
send the Holy Spirit to guide the church and its leaders,
and that the bishops' united teaching is more reliable than
the limited, private judgment of any individual member of
the church.

More positively, Catholics who are seeking to live a full
Christian life usually do not see the teachings of their
Church as burdensome, but welcome them as aids and
guides to living the gospel more fully. Catholics recognize
these teachings as outgrowths or applications of biblical
principles that enable them to worship and obey God more
fully. For example, consider the obligation of Catholics to
attend mass every week on Sunday, the Lord's day. This
requirement is based on scripture (Acts 2:46-47; Heb
10:25) and on many early Christian writings that consider
worship together on the Lord's day as an essential part of
Christian life.

I, personally, see God's wisdom in continuing to give
authority to the human leaders of the church. He has raised
up leaders to interpret that inspired book, the Bible, and to
apply its teaching to our lives. One is saved by hearing
God's word and doing it—not only the word that comes to
us in the Bible, but also in his word that comes to us
through the elders who teach and guide God's people by
the grace and wisdom of the Holy Spirit. Obeying the laws
of the church is also a way of obeying God, and is thereby
important for salvation.

Knowledge of Salvation

There is a basic truth in the belief of many Christians
that we can be assured of our salvation when we accept
Jesus Christ as our Lord and Savior and commit our lives to
following him. The Bible teaches that if we have committed
our lives to Jesus Christ and have decided to live in his ser-

vice, God gives us a firm hope and confidence that we will be saved. In many places, the apostle Paul speaks of the Holy Spirit as the "first-fruits" (Rom 8:23) or "down-payment" of the salvation that Jesus Christ has won for us.

We rejoice in our hope of sharing in the glory of God... and hope does not disappoint us, because God's love has been poured into our hearts through the Holy Spirit who has been given us. (Rom 5:2, 5)

I personally can attest that I have a firm confidence and hope that God in his mercy will preserve me from serious sin and rebellion and will finally bring me to eternal life with him.

However, Catholic teaching makes a distinction between this "firm hope and confidence" of salvation and certain unmistakable knowledge or assurance from God that one will be saved. The Catholic Church has always taught that no one can know with absolute certainty in this life whether he or she will be saved, except in the rare case that a person receives a special direction revelation from God. This teaching does not deny or question God's power to save or to forgive our sins: Catholics believe that even the worst sinner will be saved if he sincerely repents and turns to God, even at the moment of death (see the story of the "good thief" in Lk 23:39-43). Rather, this teaching is based on the recognition that any of us, at any point in life, can turn away from God and lose the hope of heaven (Ez 33:13-20). It maintains that we should not presume to know ahead of time that we will persevere in faith until the end. The Council of Trent expressed the official Catholic teaching in its "Decree on Justification":

As regards the gift of perseverance of which it is written: He that "shall persevere to the end shall be saved" (Mt 10:22, 24:13)... let no one promise himself anything as certain with absolute certitude, although all ought to place and repose a very firm hope in God's help. For God, unless men be wanting in His grace, as He has begun a good work, so will He perfect it, "working to will and to accomplish" (Phil 2:13). Nevertheless, let those "who think themselves to stand, take heed lest they fall" (1 Cor 10:12), and "with fear and trembling work out their salvation" (Phil 2:12) in labors, in watchings, in almsdeeds, in prayers and oblations, in fastings and chastity (cf. 2 Cor. 6:3ff.)...[17]

This teaching is based on a number of passages in the New Testament that refer to the knowledge of our salvation. In the Gospel of John, Jesus promises salvation to all who truly believe in him (Jn 3:16, 5:24, 11:26, 17:3). He also says that "the man who loves his life loses it, while the man who hates his life in this world preserves it to life eternal" (Jn 12:25). He assures the apostles, who have lived out this call, that he is going ahead of them to prepare a place for them in the kingdom (Jn 14:1-4).

In the Synoptic Gospels, Jesus tells an inquirer that the way for him to obtain everlasting life is to keep the commandments, and then sell all that he has, give it to the poor, and follow him (Mt 19:16-21; Mk 10:17-22; Lk 18:18-23). Jesus assures Peter that everyone who has left behind their family and home for the sake of the Kingdom of God will receive blessings in this age and everlasting life in the age to come (Mk 10:29-31; Mt 19:29-30; Lk 18:28-30). However, Jesus warns that it is necessary to persevere in this radical call, especially in the last days. He says, "he who endures to the end will be saved" (Mk 13:13; Mt 10:22). Jesus also said, "No one who puts his hand to the plough and looks back is fit for the kingdom of God" (Lk 9:62). These passages indicate that it is possible to fail to persevere to the end.

Catholics believe that the person who believes in Jesus to the extent of giving up everything, who literally "loses his life" for the sake of the Kingdom of God, and who perseveres in this call to the end of his life, is assured of salvation.

In fact, the Catholic Church officially recognizes certain persons as "saints," men and women who are believed to be enjoying eternal life with God, because the evidence about their lives shows conclusively that they have met all of these biblical "requirements" for salvation. But we who have not reached the end of our lives on earth cannot have the same assurance about our own salvation. Even though we may now have a strong faith and be laying down our lives completely for him, no one of us can be absolutely certain that we will not fall into sin or rebel against God before the end of our lives. This is equally true of every member of the church: lay people, religious, priests, bishops, and even the Pope.

Even the apostle Paul did not claim absolute certainty about his own salvation. Who could have had more reason for being sure about his own salvation than St. Paul? Who had a more dramatic and radical conversion experience? Who could claim to have given up his whole life and destiny for the sake of the Gospel more completely than Paul? But the apostle Paul refused to make any final judgment about his own salvation.

> I do not even judge myself. I am not aware of anything against myself, but I am not thereby acquitted. It is the Lord who judges me. Therefore do not pronounce judgment before the time, before the Lord comes, who will bring to light the things hidden in darkness and disclose the purposes of the heart. Then every man will receive his commendation from God. (1 Cor 4:3-5)

Elsewhere, Paul compared life in this world to a race or a fight, and himself as the athlete competing in it. Although Paul had great confidence and hope of his final victory, he made it clear that he had not yet attained his goal. He wrote:

> I wish to know Christ and the power flowing from his resurrection; likewise to know how to share in his sufferings by being formed into the pattern of his death. Thus

do I hope that I may arrive at resurrection from the dead.

It is not that I have reached it yet or have already finished my course, but I am racing to grasp the prize, if possible, since I have been grasped by Christ Jesus. Brothers, I do not think of myself as having reached the finish line. I give no thought to what lies behind but push on to what is ahead. My entire attention is on the finish line as I run toward the prize to which God calls me—life on high in Christ Jesus. All of us who are spiritually mature must have this attitude. If you see it another way, God will clarify the difficulty for you. (Phil 3:10-16)

In 1 Cor 9:26-27, Paul uses the same metaphor:

I do not run like a man who loses sight of the finish line. I do not fight as if I were shadowboxing. What I do is discipline my own body and master it, for fear that after having preached to others I myself should be rejected (or disqualified).

Paul is not the only New Testament author who wrote of the need for perseverance in faith until the end. The author of the letter to the Hebrews makes the same point. Chapters three and four of Hebrews remind Christians of the disobedience of the Hebrew people after God had called them out of bondage in Egypt; the result was that they failed to enter the promised land and instead died in the desert. Could the same thing happen to Christians today? Apparently, for the author of Hebrews says, "Let us therefore strive to enter that rest, that no one may fall by the same sort of disobedience" (Heb 4:11).

Hebrews 6 speaks even more directly of "those who have once been enlightened, who have tasted the heavenly gift and become sharers in the Holy Spirit... have tasted the goodness of the word of God and the powers of the age to come" who have now actually fallen away and are "crucify-

ing the Son of God... and hold him up for contempt"
(Heb 6:6). The author goes on to encourage his readers
that "we are persuaded of better things in your regard,
things pointing to your salvation" (Heb 6:9). God is not
unjust, the author says, and will not forget your love and
service, past and present, to his holy people. However, in
order to remind them that they have not already attained
their goal of salvation, he concludes,

> Our desire is that each of you show the same zeal till the
> end, fully assured of that for which you hope. Do not
> grow lazy, but imitate those who, through faith and
> patience, are inheriting the promises. (Heb 6:11-12)

The Book of Revelation also speaks of the need for perseverance to the end. The letters to the churches in chapters 2 and 3 encourage them to return to their "first love"
(Rv 2:4) and not fall away. The letter to the church in
Thyatira is particularly enlightening. The author praises the
church for its love and service and endurance but then
warns the community against tolerating a "Jezebel" who is
seducing God's servants. God says that he will give this
Jezebel and her followers a chance to repent and "I will
give each of you what your conduct deserves" (Rv 2:23).
The author of the Apocalypse concludes, "To the one who
wins the victory, who keeps my ways 'til the end, I will give
authority over the nations... and I will give him the morning star [Jesus Christ]" (Rv 2:26-27). May we all persevere
to the end and receive the reward of our faith and conduct—the morning star, Jesus Christ!

Peter, too, encourages Christians to wait in hopeful
expectation for the Lord's coming when "the morning star
rises in your heart" (2 Pt 1:19). In his first letter he exhorts
us to stand firm, hoping for and believing in the gift of salvation, until the Lord comes.

So gird the loins of your understanding; live soberly, set
all your hope on the gift to be conferred on you when

Jesus Christ appears. As obedient sons, do not yield to
the desires that once shaped you in your ignorance.
Rather, become holy yourselves in every aspect of your
conduct, after the likeness of the holy One who called
you; remember scripture says, "Be holy, for I am holy."
In prayer you call upon a Father who judges each one
justly on the basis of his actions. Since this is so, conduct
yourselves reverently during your sojourn in a strange
land.... So strip away everything vicious, everything
deceitful, pretenses, jealousies, and disparaging remarks
of any kind. Be as eager for milk as newborn babes—
pure milk of the Spirit to make you grow unto salvation,
now that you have tasted that the Lord is good.

(1 Pt 1:13-15; 2:1-3)

A correct Catholic understanding of salvation does not
lead to anxiety about our eternal destiny, but reminds us
that we must continually rely on God's mercy and grace for
salvation. While we cannot have absolute assurance of our
salvation, we do have great confidence that God will give us
the grace to persevere in faith and be saved—what Catholic
theology calls "the grace of final perseverance." We possess
our salvation in hope; as Paul says, "We rejoice in our hope
of sharing the glory of God" (Rom 5:2). He also says, "For
in this hope we were saved. Now hope that is seen is not
hope. For who hopes for what he sees. But if we hope for
what we do not see, we wait for it with patience." (Rom
8:24-25)

Have You Been Saved?

Evangelical Protestants will sometimes ask a Catholic
acquaintance "Have you been saved?" Many Catholics find
this a puzzling question. On the one hand, a Catholic
wants to say "of course I've been saved. Why do you have
to ask?" But on the other hand, the question seems to sug-

gest that a person's salvation is a once-and-for-all event that happens in a single moment, rather than a process or a "race" that continues throughout our lives.

I believe that a Catholic can adequately answer the question "have you been saved" by giving three different answers. The Catholic can say that, "I have been saved"; "I am being saved"; and "I hope to be saved."

First, a Catholic can say "I have been saved." It is an objective fact that Jesus Christ already has died and been raised to save me from my sin. The salvation of the world has been accomplished by Jesus Christ. This salvation has already begun to take effect in the life of everyone who has accepted Jesus Christ and been baptized. As St. Paul said, "If anyone is in Christ, he is a new creation" (2 Cor 5:17). In this sense, I can say, "Yes, I have been saved."

Secondly, Catholics need to say that "I am being saved." We must realize that we are still "running the race" to our ultimate destiny of heaven. We must turn to the Lord each day for the grace to enter more deeply into his plan for our lives and to accept his gift of salvation more fully. "And we all, with unveiled face, beholding the glory of the Lord, are being changed into his likeness from one degree of glory to another (2 Cor 3:18). In this sense, I can say, "I am being saved."

Thirdly, Catholics say that "I hope to be saved." We must persevere in our faith in God, love for God, and obedience to his will, until the end of our lives. We have hope and confidence that God will give us that grace, and that we will respond to it and accept his gift of salvation until the day we die. In this sense, "I hope to be saved." Like Paul,

I hope that I may arrive at the resurrection from the dead. It is not that I have reached it yet, or have already finished my course, but I am racing to grasp the prize if possible, since I have been grasped by Jesus Christ.

(Phil 3:11-13)

TWO

Where Do Catholic Beliefs Come From?

A S INDICATED IN THE PROLOGUE, Catholics believe that the primary mission of their church is to teach the gospel of Jesus Christ in its fullness. Thus, Catholics do not view their beliefs as something "added on" to basic Christianity, but as a faithful presentation of the "full gospel" of Jesus Christ.

But what is the "full gospel?" Where is it to be found? The first place to look is the Bible. Many Christians say that the Bible alone contains all of Christian truth. This is the principle of *sola scriptura* or "scripture alone." Catholic Christians certainly agree that the Bible is the inspired word of God and the primary source of the "full gospel" of Jesus Christ. The Second Vatican Council of the Catholic bishops affirmed boldly:

> The books of Scripture must be acknowledged as teaching firmly, faithfully and without error that truth which God wanted to put into the sacred writings for the sake of our salvation. Therefore, "all Scripture is inspired by God and useful for teaching, for reproving, for correcting, for instruction in justice; that the man of God may be perfect, equipped for every good work." (2 Tm 3:16-17)[1]

The Bible is the basis of Christian belief, and therefore of Catholic belief. It is God's revealed word or message to mankind.

However, Catholics do not believe that the Bible is the *only* source of revelation and guidance for Christians. The Bible itself does not clearly teach this. If anything, the Bible testifies that God's way of revealing himself and leading his people is to choose certain persons for these tasks, such as the patriarchs, prophets, judges, and kings of the Old Testament, and the apostles, prophets, teachers, and bishops of the New Testament. Catholics believe that throughout history God has continued to select certain individuals to lead his people and to teach with his authority. Sometimes God also leads and guides his people as a whole through the direct inspiration and work of the Holy Spirit. This is not to deny or minimize the importance of the Bible. Rather, Catholics desire to recognize and value *all* the ways that God instructs and directs the church.

In studying the history of early Christianity, Catholics observe that many of the church's beliefs and practices emerged long before the Bible was written or compiled. The Bible itself was one very important "product" of the church's life, and came to be recognized by the church as its own sacred, divinely inspired "book." But the church existed before the Bible, and literally brought it into being.

How did the Bible emerge within the church? There were a number of stages of the Holy Spirit's activity in this development. First, the Holy Spirit inspired certain authors to write what God wished to reveal to mankind. The same Holy Spirit later guided the bishops, the church's leaders, to determine which of these writings were to be accepted as divinely inspired sacred scripture. The Spirit of God also enabled the church's leaders to interpret and teach the Bible's true meaning to their congregations and to non-believers. While all of this was occurring, the Holy Spirit was also at work guiding the early Christians to develop forms of worship, prayer, community life, and so on, that were not explicitly contained in the biblical writings, and yet were important parts of God's plan for the church. Understanding all of these aspects of the Holy Spirit's guidance is important in order to appreciate where the Bible and Catholic beliefs come from.

How the Gospel of Jesus Was Proclaimed and Passed On

First of all, let us examine the development of the New Testament by briefly recounting how the Good News of Jesus Christ was first proclaimed, how it was passed on within the early Christian church, and how it has come down to us today.

Imagine that you are a Jew on pilgrimage to Jerusalem in the early 30's A.D., on your way to offer sacrifice at the temple on the Feast of Weeks or Pentecost. As you enter the city gates, you hear a commotion echoing down the narrow streets. Curious, you push your way through the gathering crowd and find a small group of men and women shouting excitedly from a balcony overlooking the street. Though dressed plainly, as Galilean hill folk, they appear to be speaking fluently in a number of languages because people from many lands seem to be understanding them. Moving closer, you hear them speaking in your own native tongue! A rough-looking, bearded man among them comes forward and speaks to the crowd: "Fellow Jews, and all of you who are in Jerusalem, let me explain this to you; listen carefully to what I say."

The speaker, of course, was the apostle Peter and the commotion in the street followed the outpouring of the Holy Spirit on the day of Pentecost. The good news of Jesus' death and resurrection was being proclaimed boldly in public for the first time.

With the coming of the Holy Spirit at Pentecost, the church of Jesus Christ was empowered to proclaim the gospel to the ends of the earth. At first, this message was not written down, but was alive in the hearts and minds of Jesus' disciples, especially the twelve. The twelve apostles were trained to understand and teach Jesus' message as no others were, for Jesus had formed them for this task and they had learned it by walking with him through times of trial and glory. So, from the beginning of Christianity, the teaching of Jesus' apostles was the most reliable source of the truth about him.

At first the teaching of the apostles was passed on by word of mouth from believer to believer, community to community. There was no need to write anything down, since people were used to remembering important stories accurately. Besides, Jesus' followers expected that he might return at any moment to establish the fullness of his kingdom.

This passing on of the good news of Jesus by word of mouth is called oral tradition. "Tradition" is not always highly regarded today, but the term simply means something that is handed over, passed on, or transmitted from one person or group to another. The original Greek word for tradition, *paradosis,* is the term that the apostle Paul used to explain how he had received the gospel of Jesus:

> "I hand on [*paredoka*] to you first of all what I myself received [*parelabon*], that Christ died for our sins in accordance with the scriptures, that he was buried and, in accordance with the scriptures, rose on the third day" (1 Cor 15:3-4).

Paul also wrote in the same way about the teaching on the eucharist: "I received [*parebalon*] from the Lord what I handed on [*paredoka*] to you, namely that the Lord Jesus on the night in which he was handed over [*paredideto*] took bread . . ." (1 Cor 11:23). Paul acknowledged that he was only teaching the "tradition," that is, what had been "handed on" to him, presumably either from the apostles or from the Lord himself. This was his guarantee of the truth of the message, and so he could assure his listeners that if they held fast to it they would be saved. He also exhorted the church in Thessalonika: "Therefore, brothers, stand firm. Hold fast to the traditions [*paradoseis*] you received from us, either by word of mouth or by letter" (2 Thes 2:15).

The letter was another way that Paul and the other apostles passed on the good news. They wrote to the churches they founded, and their letters were preserved and passed around among the churches.

Obviously the apostles themselves could not hand on the gospel to everyone in the world. There were not enough of them and they would not live forever. And so those who had received the gospel from the apostles were commissioned to hand it on themselves to others. The second letter to Timothy speaks of this: "The things which you have heard from me through many witnesses you must hand on (*parathou*) to trustworthy men who will be able to teach others" (2 Tm 2:2).

Who were these "trustworthy men" who were to be responsible for teaching the gospel? The letters to Timothy and Titus speak of different "elders" in the Christian community: bishops (*episcopoi*), presbyters (*presbyteroi*), and deacons (*diakonoi*). A bishop had to be "a good teacher" (1 Tm 3:2). The letter to Titus, another disciple of Paul, is even more explicit: "in his (the bishop's) teaching, he must hold fast to the authentic message, so that he will be able both to encourage men to follow sound doctrine and to refute those who contradict it" (Ti 1:9).

In the early church the bishop was the elder with the primary responsibility for proclaiming and defending the authentic message of Jesus in each local Christian church. Many early Christian writings attest to this. For example, in the year 96 A.D., just 30 years after Paul's death, the church in Corinth received a stern letter from Clement, who was an elder (and probably bishop) of the church in Rome.[2] Clement rebuked a certain group of Christians who were trying to overthrow the legitimate elders of the church in Corinth. Clement argued that just as God sent Jesus and as Jesus chose the apostles, the apostles "appointed their first converts, after testing them by the Spirit, to be bishops and deacons of future believers."[3]

These men were entrusted with the duty of proclaiming the gospel. According to Clement, the apostles also taught that when those they appointed died "other approved men should succeed to their ministry."[4] Thus, Clement recognized that the gospel was to be passed on through an unbroken succession of elders, originating with the apostles themselves. He told the community that they should correct those men who were challenging the authority of the legitimate bishops and elders.

In 110 A.D., Ignatius, the bishop of Antioch, was marched to Rome to be martyred. He wrote letters to many Christian churches along the way and, in each letter, he urged the people to respect and obey their bishop as they would Jesus Christ. For example, he wrote to the church at Tralles: "When you obey the bishop as if he were Jesus Christ, you are (as I see it) living not in a merely human fashion but in Jesus Christ's way. . . . It is essential, therefore, to act in no way without the bishop, just as you are doing."[5]

Why did these early Christian leaders place such importance on the authority of bishops? One of the major reasons was that bishops safeguarded the gospel of Jesus Christ. As Paul warned Timothy, there were many false teachers who were attempting to distort the true faith (1 Tm 1:1-7; 2 Tm 2:14-19, 3:1-9). In about 185 A.D., Irenaeus, bishop of Lyons (in what is now France), defended the faith against false teachers by tracing the true gospel back to its roots in the teaching of the apostles. He wrote: "The tradition of the apostles, made clear in all the world, can be seen in every church by those who wish to behold the truth. We can enumerate those who were established by the apostles as bishops in the church, and their successors down to our time, none of whom taught or thought of anything like their mad ideas."[6]

Irenaeus then traced the succession of bishops in "that very great, oldest, and well-known church founded and established at Rome by those two most glorious apostles, Peter and Paul."[7] The church at Rome was actually well established when

Paul arrived there as a prisoner, and it had a position of special importance in the early church because both Peter and Paul had given their final teaching to the elders and bishops in Rome. As Irenaeus put it: "For every church must be in harmony with this church [Rome], because of its outstanding pre-eminence, that is, the faithful from everywhere, since the apostolic tradition is preserved in it by those from everywhere."[8]

In summary, historians generally agree that by the middle of the second century each local Christian community was led by a single bishop.[9] The bishop was primarily responsible for defending and passing on the genuine apostolic tradition about the life and teaching of Jesus Christ. The bishop rebuked false teachers, maintained unity in the local church by serving as its chief shepherd, and was the official spokesman of the local community in the broader church. After the death of the apostles, the bishops' recognized teaching office ("magisterium" in Latin) became the first important vehicle for passing on and defending the true gospel of Jesus.

The Development of the New Testament

But what about the Bible? Isn't the Bible the primary source of the authentic apostolic teaching about Jesus? It is, but the New Testament that we have went through a long process of development in which tradition and the bishops have played an essential role.

The good news of Jesus Christ was first spread by word of mouth and then by the letters of the apostles. When Christians realized that the second coming of Jesus might not occur immediately and that the events of his life might be forgotten or distorted, they began to write down short accounts of parts of Jesus' ministry. This "written tradition" probably began with accounts of Jesus' death and resurrection, then with reports of his miracles, parables, and teachings, and finally with stories of his birth and childhood. But there is little evidence that a complete gospel containing all of these elements existed until after 60 A.D.

When Christians did compile these gospels, they were discerned and tested. This, in fact, was one of the most important tasks of the bishops and elders of the early church. If you were a Christian in Ephesus in the mid-70's A.D. you can imagine the excitement that would greet the news that someone has just delivered a manuscript of the complete life and teachings of Jesus! But the elders of the church would receive the parchments with caution along with gratitude. They would have been aware that a number of collections of Jesus' sayings had been circulated, some of them rather strange and unorthodox. But this manuscript looks different. It begins with the statement that it was written by Luke, a companion of Paul, for a learned Greek interested in Christianity. It begins:

Many have undertaken to compile a narrative of the events that have been fulfilled in our midst, precisely as those events were *handed on* (*paredosan*) to us by the original eye-witnesses and ministers of the word. I too have carefully traced the whole sequence of events from the beginning, and have decided to set it in writing for you, Theophilus, so that your Excellency may see how reliable the instruction was that you received. (Lk 1:1-4)

The bishops of Ephesus and nearby churches would prayerfully discern and discuss this manuscript. Over time, they would agree that this account of Jesus' life is in harmony with the traditions that they have received from the apostles. Although Luke is not himself an eye-witness or "minister of the word," the elders would eventually agree that the account of Jesus' life that Luke compiled from the testimony of those earlier witnesses is truly inspired by the Holy Spirit.

This is how the Bible came to be. From among the many

Christian writings being circulated, the bishops had to determine which ones faithfully conveyed the apostles' teaching and which did not. Over the course of many years, bishops developed lists of writings that they considered to be truly inspired by the Holy Spirit—the word of God for the whole church. These official lists of inspired writings were called "canons."

A canon developed by Bishop Irenaeus of Lyons around 185 A.D. is very similar to the present New Testament canon, though he never mentions 3 John, James, or 2 Peter.[10] Another canon similar to the present one is found written on the Muratorian Fragment, probably from the church of Rome about 200 A.D."[11] But even in the fourth century the question of which writings belonged in the New Testament was not really settled. In the late third century, Bishop Eusebius of Caesarea, in his *History of the Church,* refers to the letters of James, Jude, 2 Peter, and 2 and 3 John as "disputed, yet familiar to most."[12] It took centuries before the bishops of the church came to a final agreement on the complete New Testament canon as we know it. The recognition of the canon of the Old Testament by the bishops went through a similar process. In fact, Protestants and Catholics today still disagree about which books make up the Old Testament canon.

The Book of the Church

What can we learn from this? First, it is clear that the writings that we now call the New Testament were initially part of the "apostolic tradition," the teaching of the apostles about Jesus that was handed on within the church.

Secondly, the bishops and elders of the church discerned that these writings, and not others, are divinely inspired and thus have unique authority. Hence, the Bible is not something totally distinct and separate from "tradition" or from the teaching authority of the bishops. In the early church, the authority of the Bible grew up along with the teaching authority of the bishops. Ultimately, it was the bishops who discerned the truth of every tradition and teaching in the early church, including the traditions that became the canon of the Bible.

This does not mean that the bishops are above the Bible. Once the bishops agreed that the Bible had been uniquely inspired by the Holy Spirit they readily submitted themselves to it. It was the bishops' task to protect and proclaim God's word once the Holy Spirit led them to recognize what that word was. In fact, the Catholic Church teaches that no new writings can be added to the Bible. The bishops assembled at the Second Vatican Council declared that "we now await no further new public revelation before the glorious coming of our Lord Jesus Christ" (cf. 1 Tm 6:14 and Ti 2:13).[13]

Hence, the Bible is the inspired word of God and the "book of the church." It is the product of oral and written traditions that were handed on within the church, and each writing in the Bible was discerned by the church's bishops to be uniquely inspired by the Holy Spirit and to have irrefutable authority within the church.

The Authentic Interpretation of the Bible

After the church agreed that certain writings were inspired by God and belonged in the canon of the Bible, a further question arose: how are these writings to be properly interpreted? In the early church, disputes often arose among Christians about the genuine meaning and proper interpretation of the Bible. Christians who agreed on the canon of the New Testament sometimes held radically different views about what scripture taught about such things as the nature of the eucharist, the divinity of Jesus, the importance of Mary, and other important questions.

Christians still disagree on these and other important matters. One of the most important issues is the question of how the Bible is to be properly interpreted. Catholics believe that the leaders of their church, the bishops, have been given the charism (or gift) and the responsibility to interpret and correctly teach the word of God, just as in the early church the bishops were charged by God with the responsibility of determining which writings were divinely inspired. This task is an integral part of the bishops' role in the church: to maintain the unity of the church based on the truth of the gospel of Jesus Christ.

The bishops of the early church undertook this immensely important task when they met together in synods and councils to seek the guidance of the Holy Spirit together according to the model of the council of Jerusalem (see Acts 15). Many central doctrines of Christian belief were formulated at the councils of the early church. Catholics believe that the bishops continue to exercise this responsibility. The Catholic Church teaches that God guides the bishops of the church in discerning the true meaning of the scriptures, and that they cannot teach error whenever they meet together in an "ecumenical" or worldwide council and officially interpret a disputed passage of scripture. Catholic Christians understand this as God's plan for safeguarding the truth and keeping the church unified in its faith. As Jesus told the twelve at the Last Supper:

> I have yet many things to say to you, but you cannot bear them now. When the Spirit of truth comes, he will guide you into all the truth; for he will not speak on his own authority, but whatever he hears he will speak, and he will declare to you the things that are to come. (Jn 16:12-13)

These "new things" that the Holy Spirit stirs up in the church include new forms of worship, new Christian life styles, movements of renewal, and deeper understandings of Christian teaching. These innovations and new expressions of gospel truth may never contradict the teaching of the Bible; they must be rooted in biblical revelation. But, if they are discerned to be authentic, they provide a fuller understanding of Christian truth and a richer expression of Christian life. The Holy Spirit is alive in the church and is continually leading Christians into the fullness of truth. Catholics believe that the authority needed both to keep the church united and to discern what is truly from the Lord belongs particularly to the bishops. By virtue of their gifts and office, the bishops exercise that apostolic authority to guide the church in Jesus' name.

Catholics also believe that the teaching authority is manifested in a special way in the formal teaching of the bishop of Rome, the pope. We will discuss the role of the pope more fully in a later chapter. Here it is enough to note, as the quotation from Irenaeus cited earlier attests, that Christians early on viewed the church of Rome as having a unique ministry in guarding the truth and unity of Christian teaching.

Catholic Christians today believe that their understanding of the relationship between the Bible, tradition, and church authority is the same as that which developed in the early church. This teaching is expressed fully and clearly in the *Dogmatic Constitution on Divine Revelation* of the Second Vatican Council, especially in chapter two of that document, "The Transmission of Divine Revelation." I would highly recommend reading this document for a fuller understanding of the questions raised in this chapter. I can think of no better way to conclude this chapter than to quote the conclusion of chapter two of the Dogmatic Constitution:

> Sacred scripture is the word of God as it is put down in writing under the inspiration of the Holy Spirit. And tradition transmits in its entirety the word of God which has been entrusted to the apostles by Christ the Lord and the Holy Spirit. It transmits it to the successors of the apostles so that they may faithfully preserve this word of God, explain it, and make it more widely known. . . .
>
> The task of authentically interpreting the word of God, whether in its written form or in the form of tradition, has been entrusted exclusively to the living teaching office of

the church, whose authority is exercised in the name of Jesus Christ. This teaching office is not above the word of God, but serves it, teaching what has been handed on, listening to it devoutly, guarding it scrupulously, and explaining it faithfully by divine commission and with the help of the Holy Spirit; it draws from this deposit of faith everything which it presents for belief as divinely revealed.

It is clear, therefore, that sacred tradition, sacred scripture, and the teaching authority of the church, in accord with God's most wise design, are so linked and joined together that one cannot stand without the others, and that all together and each in its own way under the action of the Holy Spirit contribute effectively to the salvation of souls.[14]

THREE

The Church: How Catholics Understand It

T HE ACTS OF THE APOSTLES reports that in Antioch the followers of Jesus Christ were first called "Christians" (Acts 11:26). These followers of Jesus were not isolated individuals. As the Second Vatican Council taught: "It has pleased God, however, to make men holy and save them not merely as individuals, without any mutual bonds, but by making them into a single people, a people which acknowledges him in truth and serves him in holiness."[1] As Peter wrote, "Once you were no people, but now you are God's people; once there was no mercy for you, but now you have found mercy" (1 Pt. 2:10). The New Testament often calls this people, the community of disciples of Jesus Christ, the "church" (Gal 1:13; Acts 8:1; Eph 1:15, 22; Col 1:18). Even Jesus used this term (Mt 16:18, 18:17). But what is the church? Where is the church of Jesus Christ to be found today?

This chapter will explore some aspects of how Catholic Christians understand the church. For a fuller view, interested readers should begin by studying the *Dogmatic Constitution on the Church,* the central decree of the Second Vatican Council. The classic Catholic understanding of the church is summarized in the statement that the church is one, holy, catholic, and apostolic. Let us now examine these scriptural characteristics or "marks" of the church.

The Church Is One

Catholics believe that God wills there to be one united church. In John's Gospel, Jesus prays fervently that all his followers would be one, even as he and the Father are one (Jn 17:20, 21). "I have given them the glory you gave me that they may be one, as we are one, that their unity may be complete. So shall the world know that you sent me" (Jn 17:22, 23). The letter to the Ephesians exhorts Christians to

> make every effort to preserve the unity which has the Spirit as its origin and peace as its binding force. There is but one body and one Spirit just as there is but one hope given all of you by your call. There is one Lord, one faith, one baptism, one God and Father of all. (Eph 4:3-6)

The verse preceding this passage reveals the only way that this unity can be maintained: "live a life worthy of the calling you have received, with perfect humility, meekness, and patience, bearing with one another in love" (Eph 4:1, 2).

The early Christians understood the importance of this unity. Christianity spread rapidly throughout the Roman Empire; the apostles everywhere established "churches"— local groups of those who believed in Jesus Christ and who respected the apostolic authority that Jesus had established. Those groups understood themselves as local units of the one, universal church of Jesus Christ. They referred to themselves as "the church *in* Philippi," or "the church *in* Corinth" to underscore that they were local expressions of one, universal (or "catholic") church of Christ.

A careful reading of the New Testament will reveal the

lengths to which the early Christians went to preserve the unity of the church. For example, the apostle Paul wrote to the church in Philippi:

> Conduct yourselves, then, in a way worthy of the Gospel of Christ. If you do, whether I come and see you myself or hear about you from a distance, it will be clear that you are standing firm in unity of spirit and exerting yourselves with one accord for the faith of the gospel.... I beg you, make my joy complete by your unanimity, possessing the one love, united in spirit and ideals. (Phil 1:27, 2:2)

Paul not only taught this, but strove mightily for the unity of the church in his own ministry. He travelled to Jerusalem so that the elders there could confirm the accuracy of his presentation of the Gospel (Gal 2:1, 2). He journeyed again to Jerusalem for a council of elders (Acts 15), which met to seek a united teaching on the requirements for Gentiles to enter the church. He took up a collection in Gentile lands for the Jerusalem church, both to aid that church and to show solidarity with the Jewish Christians there. Paul did not always agree with the actions of other leaders of the church; he even corrected Peter for vacillating on an important issue (Gal 2:11ff.) but he never denounced Peter's role of leadership in the church. From the evidence we have, Paul never attempted to undermine Peter's role nor tried to form his own church; there was no "church of Paul" as distinct from the "church of Peter." Paul expressed his position clearly when he upbraided the Corinthians for such divisions:

> For it has been reported to me by Chloe's people that there is quarrelling among you, my brethren. What I mean is that each one of you says, "I belong to Paul," or "I belong to Apollos," or "I belong to Cephas [Peter]," or "I belong to Christ." Is Christ divided? Was Paul crucified for you? Or were you baptized in the name of Paul? (1 Cor 1:11-13)

Catholic Christians firmly believe that God intended there to be one church, with Jesus Christ as its cornerstone (Eph 2:20) and head (Eph 1:22).

The Church Is Catholic

The Apostles' Creed and other early Christian professions of faith express a belief in "the holy catholic church." What does the term "catholic" mean, and where did it come from? Literally, the word means "universal," "all-embracing," or "all-inclusive." The term refers to one church that would embrace *all* who followed Jesus Christ.

The first recorded use of the term "catholic church" is in a letter that Bishop Ignatius of Antioch wrote to the church at Smyrna shortly before his martyrdom in 110 A.D. Ignatius, one of the leading bishops of the church at this time, wrote, "Where the bishop is present, there let the congregation gather, just as where Jesus Christ is, there is the catholic church."[2] Ignatius used the term "catholic'" in its usual meaning of "total" or "universal." His point was that the bishop is the focal point of unity of the local church or congregation, just as Jesus Christ is the focal point of unity of the "whole," "total" or "universal" church. For Ignatius, "catholic" church simply meant "the whole church" or "the universal church."

However, the phrase "catholic church" acquired a different meaning in the second and third centuries. Some Christians became convinced that the "universal church" led by the recognized bishops was not the true church of Jesus Christ. Some of them broke away from the universal church and started their own churches. These churches included the Montanists in the second century; the Arians, a fourth century group which denied the divinity of Jesus; and the Donatists, a church in north Africa.

The bishops of the "original" church of Jesus Christ distinguished themselves from these other churches by calling their church the "catholic church." "Catholic" no longer meant "the total church" because not everyone who claimed to be Christian belonged to the catholic church. The catholic church was still by far the largest and most nearly universal church, but it was no longer the "total church." "Catholic" thus became like a first name, describing the type of Christian one was. That is why in this book I often refer to "Catholic Christians," because Catholics are Christians who identify themselves by the first-name "Catholic" in order to distinguish themselves from other Christian groups.

This use of "catholic" has ancient roots. In his *Confessions* (written between 397 and 401 A.D.), Augustine says that his mother Monica told him shortly before she died that "I did have one reason for wanting to live a little longer: to see you become a Catholic Christian before I died."[3] Monica's prayers were answered, and Augustine became one of history's greatest spokesmen and defenders of the Catholic Christian church. Augustine and other bishops eventually vanquished the Montanists, Arians, and other breakaway churches. Nevertheless, these early struggles left the early church of Jesus Christ with a new name, "the Catholic Church."

The faith of the "catholic" church eventually became the official religion of the Roman Empire. This was another change of great importance, and it is worth digressing a bit to take up one more historical note.

It has been said that the "catholic" church was a creation of the Roman Emperor Constantine and, further, that Christianity began a great decline with his reign. The issues involved here are complex and this is not the place to examine them fully. I would, however, make a few points. First, the church had been calling itself "catholic" long before Constantine, and it already had a spiritual unity that had nothing to do with Constantine's political activities or influence. Secondly, it is an inaccurate oversimplification to view the reign of Constantine as the beginning of decline for the church. Christians had been pleading for an end to persecution for more than two hundred years before Constantine became emperor. Christians had also been earnestly praying for the Lord to raise up a Christian emperor. Constantine seemed to be the answer to these prayers. He attributed his military victories to Jesus Christ, removed all political restrictions on Christians and passed legislation favorable to Christianity, and viewed Christianity as a significant potential source of unity for the Empire. Christians rejoiced at Constantine's actions. In his famous *History of the Church,* Bishop Eusebius of Caesarea saw Constantine's accession as the climactic moment of God's vindication of the Christian people after almost 300 years of sporadic oppression and persecution.[4]

It is true that Constantine's reign marked the beginning of many new problems and challenges for the church. Constantine and his successors attempted to forge an alliance between the church and the state, often manipulating the church and its leaders in the process. "Cultural Christianity" arose as it gradually became more politically convenient to be a Christian than to be a pagan. Whether the new challenges for the church under Constantine and his successors were worse than the persecutions and other problems under the pagan emperors is a matter of historical judgment. The church's problems were certainly different after Constantine. In many ways Christianity was much better off. At the very least, it is a gross oversimplification to claim that the church began a great decline or departed radically from the true gospel of Jesus Christ beginning with the rule of Constantine.

The Church's Division and Restoration

The church that called itself the Catholic Church was by far the largest and most influential body of Christians for at least the first ten centuries after Jesus Christ. Catholic Christians today believe that the division of the one church of Jesus Christ is a great tragedy, and grieves the "heart" of God.

The first great division of Christianity was the rift between the church of the eastern part of the Roman empire and the church of the west. This division took centuries to develop. It culminated in the great schism of 1054 A.D. which divided vast numbers of "Orthodox" Christians in the east from the "Catholic Church" in the west. The western church eventually became known as "Roman Catholic" because these Christians recognized the bishop of Rome as the focal point of their unity.

The second great rift in Christianity was the division of the church at the Protestant Reformation in the sixteenth century. The Protestant reformers perceived real abuses in certain church practices and popular teachings; indeed, the Council of Trent largely accepted Martin Luther's call for reform. But for many reasons, some of them historical and political, the outcome of the Reformation was further division of the church. The Catholic Church today acknowledges that "men of both sides were to blame" for this division.[5]

The Catholic Church views these divisions in the Body of Christ as objectively sinful. The Second Vatican Council teaches:

Without doubt, this discord openly contradicts the will of Christ (Jn 17:21), provides a stumbling block to the world, and inflicts damage on the most holy cause of proclaiming the good news to every creature.[6]

The Council accepted responsibility for its share of the blame for these divisions and stated, in the name of the whole Catholic Church, "in humble prayer, we beg pardon of God and of our separated brethren, just as we forgive those who trespass against us."[7]

Ecumenism

Today, Catholic Christians are engaged actively in seeking to restore unity among Christians. This movement, "fostered by the grace of the Holy Spirit, for the restoration of unity among all Christians," is called the ecumenical movement. It includes all "those who invoke the triune God and confess Jesus as Lord and Savior."[8]

Ecumenism is not an option for Catholic Christians today. The Second Vatican Council called all Catholics to work and pray for the restoration of the unity of the church. The "Decree on Ecumenism" spelled out the Catholic Church's approach to other Christians. This document takes pains to reassure Christians who might fear that Catholic ecumenism is only a disguised way to lure other Christians back to the Catholic Church. The Second Vatican Council does not make a dsitinction between a "true church" (the Catholic Church), and other "false churches," but the bishops of the Council preferred to speak of a *fullness* of the means of the grace and salvation present in the Catholic Church, with other Christian churches or ecclesial communities having some share in that fullness. This means that Catholics can honestly approach other Christians as brothers and sisters in Christ, without necessarily having in mind "bringing them back to the fold" of the Catholic Church. Witnessing to the fullness of grace and truth to be found in the Catholic Church is certainly not precluded, but this activity is clearly distinguished by Vatican II from the work of ecumenism. Let us look at what the Catholic Church actually teaches about ecumenism and the nature of the church.

The "Decree on Ecumenism" shows the Catholic Church's respect for other Christians: ". . . All those justified by faith through baptism are incorporated into Christ. They therefore have a right to be honored by the title of Christian, and are properly regarded as brothers in the Lord by the sons of the Catholic Church."[9]

As for the nature of the church, Catholics believe that the church of Christ truly exists (or "subsists") in the Catholic Church. Vatican II's "Dogmatic Constitution on the Church" states that: "This Church (the unique Church of Christ which in the Creed we avow as one, holy, catholic, and apostolic) subsists in the Catholic Church, which is governed by the successor of Peter and by the bishops in union with that successor . . ."[10] The Vatican's "Sacred Congregation for the Doctrine of the Faith" clarified this in its Declaration "Mysterium Ecclesiae" (June 24, 1973), when it stated that, "Catholics are bound to profess that through the gift of God's mercy they belong to that Church which Christ founded and which is governed by the successors of Peter and the other apostles. . . ."[11] This statement affirms that Jesus Christ founded a real, historical church, and that Catholics belong to this church founded by Jesus and governed by the successors of Peter and the other apostles.

The Catholic Church is a full and authentic realization in history of the church of Christ. However, the Second Vatican Council also states that many elements and endowments of the church of Christ and even the grace of salvation may be found outside of the Catholic Church, especially in other Christian churches and ecclesial communities. The "Dogmatic Constitution on the Church" states that "many elements of sanctification and truth can be found outside of her [the Catholic Church's] visible structure."[12] "The Decree on Ecumenism" states that the worship and liturgical actions of other Christian bodies "can truly engender a life of grace and can be rightly described as capable of providing access to the community of salvation."[13]

A Protestant leader, Samuel McCrea Cavert, examined the "Decree on Ecumenism" and came to these conclusions:

The promise of a new era is especially evident in the new way in which the Decree speaks of non-Catholic Christians. No one can read it without being impressed by the respect shown for those outside of the Roman obedience and by the care which is taken to understand their position and to state it fairly. Moreover, instead of dogmatically insisting on their return to Rome as the only possible movement toward unity, the Decree is concerned with a movement toward Christ. From a Protestant angle, this fresh orientation is of the highest consequence and is pregnant with creative possibilities.[14]

A leading Catholic ecumenist, Fr. Kilian McDonnell, agrees that the "Decree on Ecumenism" clearly replaces the "return to Rome" approach that Catholic previously took with an approach of encouraging all Christians (including Catholics) to move forward together on the basis of the common faith we share in Jesus Christ, and honestly seeking reconciliation for past offenses.[15]

How will the restoration of the unity of the church come about? When will it happen? What will the "restored" church look like? The "Decree on Ecumenism" directs Catholics to work for Christian unity, but to leave the accomplishment of unity to God:

> This most sacred synod desires that the initiatives of the sons of the Catholic Church, joined with those of the separated brethren, go forward without obstructing the ways of divine Providence and without prejudging the future inspiration of the Holy Spirit.
>
> Further, this Synod declares its realization that the holy task of reconciling all Christians in the unity of the one and only Church of Christ transcends human energies and abilities. It therefore places its hope entirely in the prayer of Christ for the Church, in the love of the Father for us, and in the power of the Holy Spirit. "And hope does not disappoint because the love of God is poured forth in our hearts by the Holy Spirit who has been given to us."[16]

The Catholic Church believes that it has a special role of leadership in the work of ecumenism. This is primarily because of the special gift and commission the Lord has given to the Catholic Church to proclaim and preserve the fullness of the Gospel message and all of the means of salvation that Jesus established. As the Decree on Ecumenism put it, ". . . it is through Christ's Catholic Church alone, which is the all-embracing means of salvation that the fullness of the means of salvation can be obtained."[17] Thus, Catholics have the responsibility openly and lovingly to share this fullness with other Christians, that they might grow in grace and knowledge of the truth of Christ.

However, this sharing is not just a "one-way street." Catholics can also be strengthened in their faith and living of the Gospel by the witness of other Christians, as the Decree on Ecumenism also reminds us. "Nor should we forget that whatever is wrought by the grace of the Holy Spirit in the hearts of our separated brethren can contribute to our own edification. Whatever is truly Christian never conflicts with the genuine interests of the faith; indeed, it can always result in a more ample realization of the very mystery of Christ and the Church."[18]

A Holy Church That Embraces Sinners

The Catholic Church possess the fullness of God's truth and grace, and yet its leaders and members appear to be no holier than other Christians in their conduct. As the Decree on Ecumenism explains:

> For although the Catholic Church has been endowed with all devinely revealed truth and with all means of grace, her members fail to live by them with all the fervor they should. As a result, the radiance of the church's face shines less brightly in the eyes of our separated brethren and of the world at large, and the growth of God's kingdom is retarded.[19]

Catholics profess in the Apostles' and Nicene creeds that the church is holy. This raises the question of how a church of sinners claims to be a "holy" church. Catholic Christians believe that the church is holy, not by the merits or virtues of its members, but because God has called it holy. "You are a chosen race, a royal priesthood, a holy nation, God's own people" (1 Pt 2:9). This is what Paul says in the letter to the Ephesians:

> Christ loved the church and gave himself up for her, that he might make her holy, having cleansed her by the washing of water and the word, that he might present the church to himself in splendor, without spot or wrinkle or any such thing, that she might be holy and without blemish.
>
> (Eph 5:25-27)

Catholic Christians believe that the church is holy because Jesus Christ has come and died to cleanse the church of its sin—until it is at last prepared as a spotless bride for himself on the day of "marriage of the Lamb" (Rv 19:7) at the end of time.

In other words, to say that the church is holy does not mean that it is perfect, without sin. Holiness is a gift of God to his people, a share in his divine nature. As Paul taught, "we have this treasure in earthen vessels, to show that the transcendent power belongs to God and not to us" (2 Cor 4:7). By God's gift, the church is holy in this sense, but the members of the church are still sinners. Jesus taught his followers to pray, "forgive us our trespasses, as we forgive those who trespass against us" (Mt 6:12). This prayer only makes sense if there was still sin in the church. Jesus meant it when he said "it is not the healthy that need a physician, but the sick. I have not come to call the righteous, but sinners to repentance" (Mt 9:13). The first letter of John comments, "if we say we have no sin, we deceive ourselves." (1 Jn 1:8).

Therefore, there is no contradiction when Catholic Christians claim to be a holy church, and also a church of sinners. But this does not mean that Catholics comfortably accept the presence of sin in the church. As the apostle Paul wrote:

> Do not, therefore, let sin rule your mortal body and make you obey its lusts; no more shall you offer the members of

your body to sin as weapons of evil. Rather, offer yourselves to God as men who have come back from the dead to life, and your bodies to God as weapons for justice. Sin will no longer have power over you, you are now under grace, not under the law.

What does this teach us? Just because we are not under the law but under grace, we are free to sin? By no means!

(Rom 6:12-15)

God detests sin; his only Son died on the cross because of our sin. However, sin is not overcome in our individual lives immediately. God's work of rooting out sin, both in individuals and in the church, is a process that takes a lifetime. Catholics believe that sin will not be conquered totally until Jesus comes again in glory to complete his work of purifying the church and to judge all men. Until then, the church is like a "pilgrim" in this world. It has not yet reached its final destination of complete freedom from the bondage of sin and of union with God, but it is ever pressing onward to this goal. The Second Vatican Council summarizes the present situation of the church in these words:

While Christ, "holy, innocent, undefiled" (Heb 7:26) knew nothing of sin (2 Cor 5:21), but came to expiate only the sins of the people (cf. Heb 2:17), the Church, embracing sinners in her bosom, is at the same time holy, and always in need of being purified and incessantly pursues the path of penance and renewal.

The Church "like a pilgrim in a foreign land, presses forward amid the persecutions of the world and the consolation of God," announcing the cross and death of the Lord until he comes (cf. 1 Cor 11:26).[20]

The Scandal of Sin in the Church

In light of this, the Catholic Church renounces "triumphalism"—the attitude that Catholics are better than other Christians. The Second Vatican Council stated many times that the Catholic Church is continually in need of repentance and renewal.

> Christ summons the Church, as she goes her pilgrim way, to that continual reformation of which she always has need, insofar as she is an institution of men here on earth. Therefore, if the influence of events or of the times has led to deficiencies in conduct, in church discipline, or even in the formulation of doctrine (which must be carefully distinguished from the deposit of faith itself), these should be appropriately rectified at the proper moment.[21]

It is always painful to recognize the presence of sin in the church, especially among its leaders, such as the bishops and popes. No Catholic could honestly deny that there have been leaders of the church who have been notable public sinners. But we gain perspective on this fact by looking at Jesus' apostles. Peter publicly denied that he knew Jesus Christ, not once but three times! And yet, Peter repented and the Lord used him as a foundation stone of the church (Eph 2:20; Mt 16:18; Lk 22:31-32). Thomas doubted that the Lord had risen until he saw for himself, but then professed, "My Lord and my God" (Jn 20:24-28). And Judas betrayed Christ and hung himself. (Did God make a mistake in choosing Judas?)

The lesson to draw from this is that no Christian, and no Christian leader, is above human weakness and personal sin. Catholics believe that God has chosen and used the bishops and popes through the ages but that these men are also sinners and "earthen vessels." Their authority comes from God, not from themselves or from any man. If God chose sinful men such as Peter, and sinful women such as Mary Magdalene, to play a leading role in the development of the church, should we be surprised that he continues to use church leaders who sometimes fall into sin?

This is not to excuse sin. But this perspective on sin is rooted in scripture. As the Second Vatican Council recognized: "Since we all truly offend in many things (cf. Jas 3:2), we all need God's mercy continuously and must daily pray: 'Forgive us our debts'" (Mt 6:12).[22] The Catholic Church teaches that "all have sinned and fall short of the glory of God" (Rom 3:23). There is no sinless, perfect church until Jesus comes again to purify it. There are no sinless, perfect Christian leaders. The approach of the Catholic Church is to acknowledge its own sin, to repent, and to seek God for the grace of purification and renewal. Vatican II insisted that this approach must mark the relationships between Catholics and other Christians:

> In ecumenical work, Catholics must assuredly be concerned for their separated brethren . . . but [Catholics'] primary duty is to make an honest and careful appraisal of whatever needs to be renewed and achieved in the Catholic household itself, in order that its life may bear witness more loyally and luminously to the teachings and ordinances which have been handed down from Christ through the apostles. . . .
>
> Every Catholic must therefore aim at Christian perfection (cf. James 1:4; Rom 12:1-2), and, each according to his station, play his part so that the church, which bears in her own body the humility and dying of Jesus (cf. 2 Cor 4:10; Phil 2:5-8), may daily be more purified and renewed, against the day when Christ will present her to himself in all her glory, without spot or wrinkle (cf. Eph 5:27).[23]

Holiness is the call and goal of all Catholic Christians. The "Dogmatic Constitution on the Church" devotes an entire chapter to "The Call of the Whole Church to Holiness," in which every member of the Catholic Church (lay person, priest, pope, religious) is exhorted to heed God's call to attain Christian perfection and holiness through the grace and gospel of Jesus Christ. "Become holy yourselves in every aspect of your conduct, after the likeness of the holy One who

called you; remember scripture says, 'Be holy, for I am holy'"
(1 Pt 2:15-16).

While all Catholics are sinners, the holiness of the Catholic
Church is also evident and manifest in the lives of so many of its
members throughout its history. The Catholic Church publicly recognizes and acclaims the witness of extraordinary
holiness through the canonization of saints. Every year, the
Pope canonizes men and women whose heroic virtue bears
witness to the holiness of the church. The Catholic Church can
also point to its "living saints" in every age, like Mother Teresa
of Calcutta today, to illustrate the holiness to which all
Catholics aspire. Finally, very few churches have established
and promoted religious life as the Catholic Church has, and no
other church has the great numbers of dedicated religious
priests and sisters. Catholics magnify the Lord for this gift of
holiness evident in so many of the church's members.

We have discussed three of the four "marks" of the church: it
is one, catholic, and holy. In the next chapter, we will discuss
the final characteristic—that the church is apostolic or
founded on the apostles. But the issue of the church's holiness
discussed here raises an important question concerning
authority and leadership: If the Catholic Church is a church of
sinners, including its leaders, how can the Pope and bishops
teach with God's authority and provide a reliable guide for the
lives of Christians?

The answer is that authority and leadership in the church is a
sovereign gift of God to his people. Men do not receive
authority by their merits; neither is God-given authority
invalidated by the presence of sin in the lives of the church's
members or leaders. The leaders of the church should especially exemplify holiness and righteousness in their personal
lives, so that they can be examples to the flock of Christ, and
not cause scandal among Christians and unbelievers. However, as we shall see, their authority to teach and guide the
church comes from God himself. We will now examine how
this gift of apostolic leadership and authority was established
by Jesus Christ and passed on in the life of the church.

FOUR

Leadership and Authority in the Body of Christ

THE LAST CHAPTER focused on the church as one, holy, and catholic. Every week, Catholic Christians also proclaim in the Nicene Creed that the church is apostolic—"built on the foundation of the apostles and prophets, Christ Jesus being the cornerstone" (Eph 2:20). But what does "apostolic" mean? How is the church "built on the foundation of the apostles?"

A general meaning of apostolic is "missionary." The literal translation of the word "apostle" is "one who is sent," and a Christian apostle is one sent to proclaim the good news of Jesus Christ. Thus, the whole church is apostolic—sent to proclaim the gospel of Jesus Christ to the world.

But the term "apostolic" also has two other important meanings. The church is apostolic—founded on the apostles—because it faithfully defends and proclaims the true teaching of the apostles. The Catholic Church has always been concerned to preserve and faithfully hand on this "apostolic tradition"—the genuine teaching of the apostles.

The other specific meaning of apostolic is that the church preserves and rightly exercises the authority that Jesus gave to the apostles, and which the apostles conferred upon the elders that took their place. The Catholic Church believes it is apostolic in this sense because it can trace its line of elders and their authority directly back to the apostles in an unbroken succession for over nineteen centuries. Thus, the term "apostolic" raises the thorny issue of authority. This is such an important issue that this chapter and the next will be devoted to examining the Catholic understanding of apostolic authority. The basic question is simply: by what authority does the Catholic church teach and act? A Catholic Christian would answer: by the authority of Jesus Christ, which he gave to his apostles, and which they gave to the elders who took their place, down through the centuries. This response could be stated more completely in five separate points:

First, God the Father sent Jesus among us with full authority to proclaim and establish God's kingdom (or reign) on earth. All authority in the church ultimately comes from God through Jesus Christ.

Secondly, Jesus chose disciples, especially "the Twelve" apostles, to carry on his mission and to act with the same authority that the Father had given him.

Thirdly, the apostles appointed other men to carry on their ministry and mission. Through prayer and the "laying on of hands," the apostles called upon the Lord to give these new leaders the same authority to teach and lead the church that they had received from Jesus himself. The early Christians believed that the new leaders had indeed received this authority from God.

Fourthly, the Lord continued to confer authority to lead the church upon the successors of the men appointed by the apostles to fulfill their ministry. Thus there began an unbroken chain or succession of elders, beginning with the apostles and carried down to the present.

Fifthly, certain Christian elders assumed special roles of leadership in the church as time went on. The bishop of Rome, in particular, came to be recognized by other Christians as exercising a role of leadership among the bishops and the

Christian people very similar to the role that Peter had among the original apostles and believers.

Apostolic authority begins with Jesus. Let us examine what he told his apostles to do and how they carried on his work.

Jesus and His Apostles

The New Testament records that Jesus selected and trained certain men, especially "the Twelve," and gave them special authority to carry on his own mission. "He called the twelve together and gave them power and authority over all demons and to cure diseases, and he sent them out to preach the kingdom of God and to heal" (Lk 9:1-3). At the end of each of the four gospel accounts, Jesus appears to the eleven apostles (excluding Judas, the betrayer), and commissions them to carry on his ministry. He gave them authority to baptize, to teach, and to make disciples of all the nations (Mt 28:19-20); to "preach the Gospel to the whole creation" (Mk 16:15); to understand the scriptures and to preach repentance and the forgiveness of sins (Lk 24:45-48); and to forgive sins (Jn 20:23). The account of Jesus' message in John's gospel reveals the meaning and source of this special "apostolic" authority: "As the Father has sent me, even so I send you." And when he had said this he breathed on them, and said to them, "Receive the Holy Spirit. If you forgive the sins of any, they are forgiven; if you retain the sins of any, they are retained." (Jn 20:21-23). In all four gospels, the last act of Jesus before his ascension is to give his chosen apostles the commission and authority to carry on his ministry. In Matthew's gospel, Jesus promised them, "Lo, I am with you always, to the close of the age" (Mt 28:20).

The apostles faithfully carried out Jesus' commission. The Gospel was proclaimed to the nations; sinners repented, confessed their sins, and were baptized into Christ and his church. When Christians realized that Jesus might not return in glory in the immediate future, the church began to make provision for the future through the Holy Spirit's guidance. The apostles prepared other men to share in their ministry and to succeed them after they died. The early Christians were convinced that Jesus intended the ministry and authority of the apostles to continue in the church, even after the apostles themselves died.

The New Testament shows us how apostolic authority was passed on in the early church. Probably the earliest New Testament writing was the apostle Paul's first letter to the Thessalonians (written about 50 A.D.). Paul says: "We beg you, brothers, respect those among you whose task it is to exercise authority in the Lord and admonish you; esteem them with the greatest love because of their work" (1 Thes 5:12-13).

From a very early point, the church had leaders whose task was "to exercise authority in the Lord and admonish" Christian believers. For example, Paul addressed his letter to the church at Philippi, "to all the saints in Christ Jesus who are at Philippi, *with the bishops and deacons.*" Bishops (*episcopoi* in Greek) and deacons (*diakonoi*) literally meant "overseers" and "servants"—probably apt descriptions of their work in the church. Later, in the pastoral epistles (written in the 80's A.D.), these names were used as titles for recognized positions of leadership in the Christian community.

The office of bishop (1 Tm 3:1) specifically carried on the ministry of the apostles. In New Testament times, bishops were married men who had demonstrated their ability to manage their households well, "for if a man does not know how to manage his own household, how can he care for God's church?" (1 Tm 3:5). Later, in imitation of Jesus' single life and through the influence of the monastic movement, bishops were celibate men who devoted their energies totally to the service of God and the church. The New Testament required that a bishop be "an apt teacher" (1 Tm 3:2). Preaching and teaching were crucial tasks of leadership in the Christian community: "Let the elders who rule well be considered worthy of double honor, especially those who labor in preaching and teaching" (1 Tm 5:17). As the letter to Titus says: "In his teaching, he (the bishop) must hold fast to the authentic message (of the gospel), so that he will be able both to encourage men to follow sound doctrine and to refute those who contradict it" (Ti 1:9).

The bishop had the special responsibility of teaching the authentic gospel message, and defending it against attack and false interpretations. This was one of the most important ways that the bishops carried on the mission and ministry of the apostles.

As the early church developed, three roles or "offices" of leadership and service came to be recognized in the local Christian communities: the bishop or overseer (*episcopos*), the elders or presbyters (*presbyteroi*), and the deacons or servants (*diakonoi*). The writings of the early church demonstrate beyond question that the one who led the others and exercised "apostolic" authority in the church was the bishop. The role of the bishop assumed increasingly greater importance as time went on. Around 96 A.D., Clement (an elder and probably bishop of the church in Rome), explained to the church in Corinth that the apostles "appointed their first converts, after testing them by the Spirit, to be bishops and deacons of future believers. This was not any novelty, for scripture had mentioned bishops and deacons long before."[1]

We have more information about authority in the church from the *Didache* (or the *Teaching of the Twelve Apostles*), probably written between 100 and 110 A.D. This work indicates that there was a gradual transition from the roles of apostles, prophets, and teachers (as referred to in 1 Corinthians) to the roles of bishop and deacons. This transition was probably due to the death of the apostles and to a decline in the number of traveling charismatic prophets and teachers, who also provided leadership in the Christian communities of the first century.[2]

The author of the *Didache* welcomed this shift in leadership:

You must, then, elect for yourselves bishops and deacons who are a credit to the Lord, men who are generous, faithful, and well-tried, for their ministry to you is identical with that of the prophets and teachers. You must not, therefore, despise them, for along with the prophets and teachers they enjoy a place of honor among you.[3]

This passage implies that some members of the early Church had difficulty accepting these new roles of bishop and deacon, and needed to be reassured that they carried out exactly the same roles as the previous leaders had.

The Local Bishop

The development of basic offices of leadership in the local churches reached its final phase by the middle or late second century. By that time, every local Christian church was led by a single bishop who was assisted by presbyters (elders) and deacons (servants). This basic pattern was the only generally accepted model of local church leadership for hundreds of years. The Catholic Church has maintained it up to the present day in its three "levels" of ordained ministry: bishops, priests, and deacons.[4]

In his role as "chief shepherd" and leader of the local church, the bishop uniquely represents the single, unique headship of Jesus Christ over the universal church. The bishop does not *replace* Jesus Christ in the local community but *represents* him; the bishop carries on Jesus' shepherding role through the commission and authority that comes from Jesus alone. The priests (or presbyters) and deacons assist the bishop in carrying on Jesus' mission and ministry.

Some of the great martyrs and saints of the early church described the roles of bishop, presbyters, and deacons in their writings. The earliest and perhaps most notable was Ignatius, bishop of Antioch, who wrote letters to numerous local churches while on the way to his martyrdom in Rome in 110

A.D. Ignatius assumes that each church to which he writes has a single bishop, and exhorts the churches to obey and respect him. He wrote to the church at Tralles:

> ... when you obey the bishop as if he were Christ Jesus, you are, (as I see it), living not in a merely human fashion, but in Jesus Christ's way. .... It is essential, therefore, to act in no way without the bishop, just as you are doing. Rather submit even to the presbytery (the body of presbyters or elders) as to the apostles of Jesus Christ. .... Those too who are deacons of Jesus Christ's mysteries must give complete satisfaction to everyone. For they do not serve mere food or drink, but minister to God's church.[5]

Ignatius employs a slightly different analogy later in the same letter: "[the deacons] represent Jesus Christ, just as the bishop has the role of the Father, and the presbyters are like God's council and an apostolic band. You cannot have a church without these."[6] To the church at Smyrna, Ignatius wrote:

> You should all follow the bishops as Jesus Christ did the Father. Follow, too, the presbytery as you would the apostles, and respect the deacons as you would God's law. Nobody must do anything that has to do with the Church without the bishop's approval. You should regard that Eucharist as valid which is celebrated either by the bishop or by someone he authorizes. Where the bishop is present, there let the congregation gather, just as where Jesus Christ is, there is the Catholic Church. Without the bishop's supervision, no baptisms or love-feasts are permitted. On the other hand, whatever he approves pleases God as well.[7]

These analogies and instructions demonstrate vividly the importance of the bishop's role in the church by 110 A.D. By this date a single bishop had been established as the head of each local Christian community that Ignatius wrote. The bishop had replaced the apostles and prophets as liturgical leader and chief teacher of the local church, and he was assisted by presbyters and deacons. Not all the local Christian churches adopted this "three-tiered'" structure of ministry at the same time, but most historians agree that it was universally accepted and practiced by the middle of the second century, by about 150 A.D. Catholic Christians see God at work in this development. It is part of the fulfillment of Jesus' promise to guide his church and preserve it in truth and unity through the Holy Spirit (Jn 16:12-15).

The Bishops and the Unity of the Church

The bishops of the local churches had a responsibility for the entire (catholic) church of Jesus Christ. Like the apostles they succeeded, the bishops viewed themselves as a body of men who were charged with the mission of spreading the gospel and of leading the church in unity. They knew that there is only "one Lord, one faith, one baptism" (Eph 4:5) and one church of Jesus Christ (Eph 4:4, 13; Jn 17:20-21).

Historian John de Satge has described the role of the bishop in providing unity in the early church in this way:

The Church was defined in the groups of people in a particular place who met around their bishop. The bishop represented Christ who was believed to be present in the local gathering. And Christ was not many but one. There was thus a hidden ("mystical") unity which meant that members of the geographically separated churches belonged to the one church. The one church was localized in many churches. The bishop around whom the local church gathered was also the representative of the universal episcopate (the universal office of bishop).[8]

How did the bishops of the early church express their spiritual unity in a practical way? In their correspondence with each other the bishops discussed questions and common problems about the Christian faith, church discipline, and order. They often compared creeds, summaries of Christian belief. They sought agreement and unity on these matters through the guidance of the Holy Spirit.

The bishops also sought unity by meeting together in regional or worldwide ("ecumenical") councils or synods, where they sought the Lord's guidance on important matters of Christian belief and practice. An account of the first major council of the church's elders is recorded in the Acts of the Apostles, Chapter 15. The issue facing the apostles and elders was the requirements necessary for Gentiles to become Christians, particularly the question of whether the Gentiles had to be circumcised and obey Jewish law. The apostles did not think that Jesus' teaching directly answered this question so they sought the guidance of the Holy Spirit. After they prayed and discussed the issue, they reached a decision and issued a letter to all the churches which stated: "It is the decision of the Holy Spirit, and ours too, not to lay on you any burden beyond that which is strictly necessary" (Acts 15:28).

The way this decision was reached and the source of its authority are of particular interest to us because the Council of Jerusalem became a model for all future ecumenical councils. The church believed that when bishops from the whole world met and solemnly decided something concerning Christian belief or the life of the church, their formal decisions and teaching were certainly true and directed by the Holy Spirit. The church saw this procedure as a practical fulfillment of Jesus' promise to his apostles to lead them into all the truth through the Holy Spirit's guidance (Jn 16:12, 13).

One of the most important aspects of Catholic belief is the conviction that God speaks with clarity and assurance about matters of faith when the recognized elders of the church meet together and seek God's wisdom and the guidance of the Holy Spirit, as we see in Acts 15. In this way, the Holy Spirit will surely lead the church into the "fullness of truth" and protect it from error. In fact, Catholic Christians have such confidence in God's faithfulness and in his will to protect the church from error that they recognize as "infallible" any official statement of an ecumenical ("worldwide") council of bishops which precisely and explicitly defines a doctrine of the Christian faith. Individuals, even individual bishops, may be wrong or deceived; groups of Christians may be wrong; but the successors of the apostles (the bishops) cannot be wrong about the Christian faith when they solemnly agree on a matter of faith or morals, and officially announce their teaching to all believers. They cannot be wrong in these circumstances because defining and protecting the faith is precisely the responsibility Jesus himself gave his apostles and their successors.

Even if the bishops do not actually meet together in an ecumenical council to discern a teaching of the Christian faith, Catholics believe that the Holy Spirit guides them and protects them from error if they agree on the teaching. As the bishops at the Second Vatican Council stated this belief:

Although the individual bishops do not enjoy the prerogative of infallibility, they can nevertheless proclaim Christ's doctrine infallibly. This is so, even when they are dispersed around the world, provided that while maintaining the bond of unity among themselves and with Peter's successor, and while teaching authentically on a matter of faith or morals, they concur in a single viewpoint as the one which must be held conclusively.

This authority is even more clearly verified when, gathered together in an ecumenical council, they are teachers and judges of faith and morals for the universal Church. Their definitions must then be adhered to with the submission of faith.[9]

Catholics view the infallibility of the united teaching of the bishops as a great gift of God to the church. Certainly it must be a gift, since no man can know the mind of God except as

God reveals it. It is a great mystery how God can use human beings as channels of his divine truth. The bishops' united teaching is a way for the truth of the Bible to be infallibly interpreted in the church down through the ages, a way for the truths that even the apostles could not yet fully understand (Jn 16:12, 13) to be unfolded in the church. The united teaching of the legitimate elders (bishops) of the church is a way God has chosen to safeguard the truth of his Word and to "announce the things to come" (Jn 16:13). Whether the bishops gather in an ecumenical council or agree at a distance upon doctrines of Christian faith and morals, Catholics accept their united teaching as a sure source of truth and unity.

Some examples of official teachings of ecumenical councils of bishops illustrate their importance. The Council of Nicea in 325 A.D. condemned Arius' denial that Jesus was fully God, equal to the Father in divinity. The Council of Constantinople in 381 A.D. affirmed that the Holy Spirit was fully God, one in being with the Father and the Son. The Council of Chalcedon in 451 A.D. taught that Jesus was both fully God and fully man. Later councils clarified important issues concerning grace and free will, salvation, the sacraments, and the nature of the church.

Those councils also decided many less important issues which were nevertheless still guided by the Holy Spirit. For example, some of the disciplinary requirements decided by the Council of Jerusalem in Acts 15 were later dropped altogether, as the situation of the church changed. Not all statements or decisions of the ecumenical councils are considered by Catholics to be infallible or permanently binding. Only those teachings which the bishops explicitly present as "dogmas" or official doctrines of faith are considered infallibly true by Roman Catholics. Hence, certain items of church law or discipline, such as fasting or abstaining from meat on certain days, may be guided by the Holy Spirit, but also liable to change if the Spirit leads the bishops differently at a later time.

In summary, we have seen that the special authority that Jesus gave his apostles to lead the church was preserved and handed on particularly through the bishops of the local Christian churches. The next chapter will examine the origins of the idea that one bishop, the pope, possesses a unique authority among the bishops for the shepherding and guidance of the church of Jesus Christ.

FIVE

The Pope: A Chief Sign of the Church's Unity

THE NEW TESTAMENT SPEAKS about bishops and their role as teachers and leaders in the church, but it does not mention the pope. Nevertheless, the Catholic belief that one man is to have an overall role of guiding and teaching the whole church is anchored in the Bible. The New Testament never uses the term "pope," but it does tell us about Simon Peter—a man whom Jesus gave a special position of leadership in the church. Peter's role is the basis and model for the leader whom Catholic Christians call the pope.

Peter and the Apostles

The New Testament provides indisputable evidence that Simon Peter had a preeminent position among Jesus' disciples and in the early church. Consider the following points:

1. In the gospels, Peter is usually the spokesman for the apostles, especially at climactic moments. (Mk 8:29; Mt 18:21; Lk 12:41; Jn 6:67ff.)

2. Peter is often the central figure relating to Jesus in dramatic gospel scenes such as walking on the water. (Mt 14:28-32; Lk 5:1ff; Mk 10:28; Mt 17:24f)

3. In the synoptic gospels, Peter is always named first when the apostles are listed (Mk 3:16-19; Mt 10:1-4; Lk 6:12-16; Acts 1:13). In fact, sometimes the apostles are referred to as simply, "Peter and his companions" (Mk 1:36; Lk 9:32; Mk 16:7).

4. In John's gospel, John waits for Peter before entering Jesus' tomb and allows him to go in first, a sign of honor and respect (Jn 20:3-8). Jesus also singled out Peter as a shepherd of God's people (Jn 21:15-17, see below).

5. Paul lists Peter as the first witness of Jesus' resurrection (1 Cor 15:5), and calls him "Cephas" (rock), the name Jesus gave him (Gal 1:18; 2:7ff, 11, 14; 1 Cor 1:12; 3:22; 9:5; 15:5).

6. In the Acts of the Apostles, Peter's leadership is acknowledged in many ways:

—Peter is the first to proclaim the gospel publicly (Acts 2:14-40).
—Peter gives many of the major speeches in Acts. (Acts 3:12-26; 4:8-12; 5:3-9, 29-32; 8:20-23; 10:34-43; 11:4-18; 15:7-11)
—The first healing miracle after Pentecost is reportedly worked through Peter's command (Acts 3:6-7), and he apparently had a widely recognized gift of healing (Acts 9:34, 38-41; Acts 5:15).
—Peter was the first to receive God's revelation that the gospel was to go to the Gentiles (Acts 10:9-48), and he was the first to command the baptism of Gentiles (Acts 10:46-48).

Then there are Jesus' explicit statements about about Peter's unique role in the church. Such sayings are found in all four gospels, indicating that all of the New Testament writers acknowledged and supported Peter's leadership role.

First, Luke's gospel reports that Jesus told Peter: "Simon,

Simon, behold Satan demanded to have you that he might sift you like wheat, but I have prayed for you that your faith may not fail; and when you have turned again, strengthen your brethren" (Lk 22:31-32). Jesus' words were fulfilled. Peter's faith in Jesus did not fail, even after he denied that he knew Christ three times. He repented and truly became a "rock" of strength for his brethren, as the passages listed above indicate.

Secondly, in John's gospel (21:15-19), Jesus asks Simon Peter three times, "do you love me?"; each time Peter affirms his love for Jesus. This is a reversal of Peter's threefold denial of Christ, but Jesus' response to Peter here is also very significant. He tells Peter, "Feed my lambs," "Tend my sheep," and finally, "Feed my sheep." Jesus calls himself "the good shepherd" in John's gospel (Jn 10:11, 14) and explains that the shepherd lays down his life for his sheep (Jn 10:11). Thus Jesus' words to Peter mean that Jesus is commissioning Peter to be the "good shepherd" who will feed and care for Jesus' flock after he departs.

Thirdly, we have Jesus' well-known statement to Peter in Mt 16:18-19 that he will build his church on this "rock." This is not the entire basis of the Catholic Christian understanding of Peter's role in the church, but it states simply and directly what all the other New Testament evidence also implies. After Peter professes that Jesus is the Messiah:

> Jesus answered him, "Blessed are you, Simon Bar-Jona (son of John)! For flesh and blood has not revealed this to you, but my Father who is in heaven. And I tell you, you are Peter [*Petros,*] and upon this rock [*petra,*] I will build my church, and the gates of Sheol will not prevail against it. I will give you the keys of the kingdom of heaven, and whatever you bind on earth shall be bound in heaven, and whatever you loose on earth shall be loosed in heaven. (Mt 16:18-19)

Books have been written about the meaning and application of this passage. What is the "rock" upon which Jesus said that he would build his church? Is it Peter? Is it Peter's faith? Or is Jesus talking about himself as the "rock?" In this short book, I can only explain how Catholic Christians have understood this passage for many centuries.

First, Jesus gives Simon a new name: *Petros* in Greek, and *Kepha* in the Aramaic spoken by Jesus and his companions. Since Matthew's gospel is written in Greek, the passage reads, "You are *Petros* and upon this *petra* I will build my church." Some people propose that since *Petros* and *petra* are slightly different forms of the word "rock," that Simon is not necessarily being identified as the "rock" (*petra*) upon which Jesus would build his church. For example, *petros* might mean a "chip of rock."

However, these two words are identical in the original Aramaic that Jesus and the Palestinian church actually spoke: "You are the *Kepha* and upon this *kepha* I will build my church." The words change in Greek because there is a gender difference in the words in the Greek language. *Petra* is feminine. Since it would be inappropriate to give Peter (the Rock) a feminine gender name, the author of the gospel simply changes it to its masculine form (*petros*), in order to apply it to Peter without embarrassment!

The Gospel also says that "upon *this* (*taute*) rock I will build my church," immediately after having called Peter "rock." This reemphasizes that *Peter* is the rock that Jesus is talking about. Most commentaries conclude that identifying the Rock as Peter's faith, or as Jesus himself, unnecessarily complicates a rather straightforward statement. "You are Peter [rock] and upon this rock I will build my church."[1]

Jesus' action in giving Simon a new name, Peter, and then explaining what it means is highly significant in the context of biblical culture. In the Bible, God gives a new name to a person or a people to mark a decisive turning-point—a new responsibility, role, or identity.[2] This fact makes the meaning of the passage even clearer. Jesus tells Simon that "you are Peter (Rock), and upon this rock I will build my church," and goes on to explain that "I will give you the keys of the kingdom of heaven." "Keys" denote authority, as in the "keys" of the city (see also Is 22:15-25; Rv 1:18). Jesus then underlined the point by explaining Peter's special authority in the kingdom of heaven, "and whatever you bind on earth shall be bound in heaven" (Mt 16:19).

Did Peter Have a Successor?

The biblical evidence strongly supports the view that Jesus gave Peter special authority. A key question, however, is whether Peter had successors. Peter may have had a leading role in the early church, but it is another matter to show that others were authorized to take over his role after he died. This is a question that Christians disagree on. Catholics believe that there is ongoing "Petrine" authority in the church, just as there is ongoing apostolic authority exercised through the bishops.

The New Testament does not report any words of Jesus that explicitly instruct the apostles or Peter to hand on their leadership or authority to others. However, Catholics believe that God established a *pattern* for leadership and authority in the church, and that the Holy Spirit continues to lead the church through this pattern.

This is, in fact, what actually happened in early Christianity. Although Jesus never explicitly mentioned "successors to the apostles," "bishops," or "deacons," the later New Testament writings tell us that the offices of bishop and deacon were recognized and accepted by Christians, with the bishops functioning as successors to the apostles in their ministry to God's people. In a similar way, the church later came to believe that the Holy Spirit desired this "Petrine" role of overall leadership and authority in the church to continue.

It should not surprise us that the Holy Spirit eventually directed the church to adopt an authority structure closely resembling the pattern Jesus established among his apostles.

The apostles worked together to guide God's people under Jesus' leadership, a leadership that Peter in some way carried on after Jesus had departed. Peter was *not* looked upon as a replacement for Jesus; he was only a visible representative of Jesus' ongoing presence and authority in the whole church, just as each local bishop came to represent the presence and authority of Jesus and the apostles in the local church. In time, the Holy Spirit led the church to recognize the need for one bishop to exercise a special role of leadership among all the bishops—just as Peter had done among the apostles. Christians in the Western part of the Roman Empire looked to the bishop of Rome to carry on this role of leadership for the whole church. In this way, the bishop of Rome became a leader in the early church much like Peter was a leader among the apostles and the first Christians. The "Petrine charism"—the gift of God to Peter—was continued in the pope.

Historical Roots of the Papacy

Why the bishop of Rome? In some ways, that is like asking, "Why Peter?" God chooses whomever he wills. But there are some historical and spiritual reasons why this choice makes sense. Rome had long been the most important city in the world—the capital and center of the Roman Empire—and it was natural to look to Rome for leadership. However, Christians also looked to Rome for a reason that had nothing to do with Rome's importance as a city. Early Christian writings stress that the church in Rome was carrying on the tradition of its two greatest Christian martyrs: the apostles Peter and Paul. An ancient and strong Christian tradition holds that both these apostles gave their final teaching in Rome and were martyred there. Thus, the bishop of Rome came to be considered the legitimate apostolic successor to the apostles Peter and Paul.

When did the bishop of Rome begin to be recognized as the successor to the apostle Peter? Many writings of the early church testify to the growing recognition of the unique leadership role of the bishop of Rome. Although a full account of these writings is beyond the scope of this book, a few of them will be considered here.

1. Before the end of the first century, the church in Rome helped to settle problems in other local churches. In 96 A.D., Clement of Rome wrote a strong letter to the church in Corinth to resolve a dispute over leadership there. The authority of this letter reminds one of Paul's letters to the Corinthian church forty years earlier.[3]

2. On his way to martyrdom in Rome in 110 A.D., the illustrious bishop Ignatius of Antioch wrote to the church in Rome:

> You are a credit to God: you deserve your renown and are to be congratulated. You deserve praise and success and are privileged to be without blemish. Yes, you rank first in love, being true to Christ's law and stamped with the Father's name.[4]

3. Around 150 A.D., the martyr-bishop Polycarp of Smyrna journeyed to Rome to confer with Pope Anicetus about the proper date for the celebration of Easter.

4. In the late second century, bishop Irenaeus of Lyons refuted false teachers by referring to "the tradition which that very great, oldest, and well-known church, founded and established at Rome by those two most glorious apostles Peter and Paul, received from the apostles . . . every church must be in harmony with this church [the church in Rome] because of its outstanding pre-eminence . . ."[5]

5. In 250 A.D., Cyprian, the martyr-bishop of Carthage in North Africa, wrote this about the one who held the "chair" or office of Peter—the bishop of Rome:

> It is on him [Peter] that He [Jesus] builds the church, and to him that He entrusts the sheep to feed. And although He

assigns power to all the apostles, yet he founded a single chair, thus establishing by His own authority the source and hallmark of the churches' oneness. No doubt the others were all that Peter was, but a primacy is given to Peter and it is thus made clear that there is but one church and one chair. ... If a man does not hold fast to this oneness of Peter, does he imagine that he still holds the faith? If he deserts the Chair of Peter upon whom the church was built, has he still confidence that he is in the church?[6]

Later Christian leaders also viewed the bishop of Rome as Cyprian did, as a "chairman" for the whole church—directing it, teaching it, and preserving its unity.

6. In the fourth century, Ambrose, the bishop of Milan who converted and baptized St. Augustine, stated: "Where Peter is, there is the church."[7] He also taught that whatever was condemned by the bishop of Rome was condemned by all.

7. Also in the fourth century, the great biblical scholar, Jerome, wrote to Pope Damasus:

I follow no one as leader except Christ alone, and therefore I want to remain in union in the church with you, that is, with the chair of Peter. I know that on this rock the church is founded."[8]

This represents the attitude of Catholic Christians throughout the ages.

8. By the fourth century, the bishop of Rome was generally recognized as the "patriarch" (or chief bishop) of the Latin-speaking or "western" part of the church. He was also first called "pope" in the mid-fourth century, a term previously used as a title of respect for bishops and superiors of monasteries. By the end of Christian antiquity (600-800 A.D.), the title "pope" was reserved for the bishop of Rome in the Western church, which recognized him as their pre-eminent spiritual leader.[9]

9. Pope Damasus, pope from 366-384 A.D., extended the influence of the papacy to local churches throughout the Roman Empire. The term "apostolic see" was then used to refer to the office of the bishop of Rome.[10]

10. During the reign of the emperor Gratian, the title of "Pontifex Maximus" (Supreme Pontiff), a title previously applied to emperors, was given to the bishop of Rome because of his leadership of the universal church.[11]

11. At the end of the Pelagian controversy, which the pope helped settle, St. Augustine stated: "Rome has spoken; the dispute is ended."[12]

12. Leo I (the Great), pope from 440-461 A.D., provided decisive teaching about Jesus Christ that guided the bishops at the Council of Chalcedon in 451 A.D. The bishops exclaimed: "Peter has spoken through Leo!" Leo also defended the city of Rome by dissuading Attila the Hun from attacking it, and later convincing Gaiseric the Vandal to sack Rome peacefully instead of destroying it.[13]

13. Gregory I (the Great), pope from 590-604, also helped maintain the political stability of the declining Roman empire, but is more noted for his vibrant missionary efforts and the unity he provided the expanding church. Gregory sent the first Christian missionaries to England, aided in the conversion of the Visigoths and the Lombards, and linked the Spanish church more closely to Rome. The pope came to be known as "the vicar of the prince of the apostles" and "the servant of the servants of God."[14]

In addition to their increasing moral and spiritual leadership, the popes after Gregory I gradually assumed greater political influence due to the instability of the times and the decline of the Roman Empire. This joining of the pope's spiritual and temporal roles of leadership eventually gave rise to "Christendom" in the middle ages—a political system in which the popes could influence the secular rulers to promote the Catholic Church and to rule according to Christian principles.

These are some of the reasons why Catholic Christians believe that the leadership role of the pope was intended by God. The Holy Spirit unfolded the role of the pope over the course of a few centuries, not overnight. Not all popes were "model Christians"; indeed, some were serious sinners. The joining of the pope's spiritual and temporal powers gave rise to some problems in the church. Nonetheless, Catholic Christians thank God for his faithfulness in raising up a scripturally rooted position of leadership through which the truths of Christianity have been faithfully preserved and passed down through the centuries to us today.

The Pope As a Christian Leader

Like all God-given authority, the pope's authority is intended for serving God's people and building up the body of Christ. Popes are not to exercise their authority for their own benefit, nor apart from the other bishops and church leaders. The apostle Peter had been a spokesman, a "rock," and a support for his fellow apostles and Christians. Consider Peter's encouraging words to his fellow elders in the church:

> So I exhort the elders among you as a fellow elder and a witness of the sufferings of Christ as well as a partaker in the glory that is to be revealed. Tend the flock of God that is your charge, not by constraint, but willingly, not for shameful gain, but eagerly, not as domineering over those in your charge, but being examples to the flock. And when the chief Shepherd is manifested you will obtain the unfading crown of glory . . . Clothe yourselves, all of you, with humility toward one another, for "God opposes the proud, but gives grace to the humble." Humble yourselves therefore under the mighty hand of God, that in due time he may exalt you. (1 Pt 5:1-6)

This passage illustrates Peter's own great humility and provides an important teaching for his successors. Peter was the head of the apostles, but he reminds the other leaders that he is also a "fellow elder" with them. The First Vatican Council affirmed this in its teaching on the relationship of the pope and the bishops:

> Rather, the power of the bishops is protected, strengthened, and upheld by the supreme and universal shepherd (the Pope), as Pope St. Gregory the Great writes: "My honor is the honor of the whole church. My honor is the solid strength of my brethren. I am truly honored when the honor due to every single one is not denied."[15]

Peter also presented himself as a servant of other Christians and a fellow believer with them. He began his second letter, "Simon Peter, a servant and apostle of Jesus Christ, to those who have obtained a faith of equal standing with ours in the righteousness of our God and Savior Jesus Christ," (2 Pt 1:1). The great Christian leaders have always professed their unworthiness to hold their positions of leadership. St. Augustine said of his role as bishop: "What I am for you terrifies me; what I am with you consoles me. For you I am a bishop; but with you I am a Christian. The former is a title of duty; the latter one of grace. The former is a danger; the latter, salvation"[16] (St. Augustine, Sermon 340, no. 1). The same is true of the office of pope. The popes have realized that they will be held accountable on the day of judgment for how well they have responded to God's call to be representatives of Christ.

For this reason, the early popes took for themselves a title that they felt best reflected their role in the church: *servus servorum Dei*—servant of the servants of God. Jesus himself said "let the greatest among you become as the youngest, and the leader as one who serves. . . . I am among you as one who serves" (Lk 22:26, 27). The image of popes "lording it over" other Christians and bishops is largely an exaggerated one; although not all popes were exemplary, most of them honestly sought to be servants of their brother bishops and of all

Christians in imitation of Jesus Christ.

Some popes, bishops and other leaders of God's people have failed to live up to this high ideal of "servant-leadership." This grieves us, but the response of faithful Catholics is not to give up on these elders, nor to leave the Catholic Church, but to pray for their pastors and support their positive leadership even more fervently. Church leaders, even the pope, are still sinners in need of redemption by Jesus Christ. Because of their positions of responsibility, they are subject to even more intense human and spiritual attack than most other Christians. They need support and prayer to fulfill their ministry. The fact that they sin is instructive. It shows us that God chooses weak and sinful men to represent him and to lead the church and that the wisdom and authority of these leaders comes from God, and not man.

The Pope's Infallibility

The pope works closely with the other bishops in proclaiming the gospel and discerning true Christian teaching. Jesus promised to send the Holy Spirit upon his apostles to guide them into the fullness of truth, and, as we saw in Chapter Four, this infallibility in the teaching of Christian truth is a gift of God to the bishops when they teach in unity.

Catholic Christians also believe that the pope himself can exercise the infallibility that God promised to the church. This belief is based, first of all, on the biblical portrait of Peter. There were times when Peter was anointed by the Holy Spirit to proclaim a truth that God wished to reveal. At Caesarea Philippi, Peter declared that Jesus was the Messiah, the Christ. When Jesus asked the apostles at that time, "Who do you say that I am?" Peter did not confer with the other apostles, but was inspired by the Holy Spirit to say, "You are the Christ" (Mk 8:29). In the Acts of the Apostles, Peter received another revelation that was crucial for the life of the early church and important for all later Christian history: that the Gentiles could be baptized to become Christians without first being circumcised. Peter did not submit his revelation to anyone else, but was led to the house of the gentile Cornelius where he understood the meaning of his vision and proceeded to baptize Cornelius and his household. These examples show that the Holy Spirit did, at times, give to Peter alone special guidance and revelation about Christian truth.

Catholics believe that at certain times in Christian history, God has spoken a similar word of sure truth through the pope, the successor of Peter, just as he spoke through Peter himself. This infallibility in teaching Christian truth is a sheer gift or charism of God for the benefit of the church; it has nothing to do with the natural wisdom, ability, or virtue of the particular man who possesses that gift through holding the office of "pope."

From the Bible we also learn that this charism of infallibility is not always operative. It is obvious that Peter did not always speak under the inspiration of the Holy Spirit, such as when he wanted to set three tents on Mt. Tabor for Jesus, Moses and Elijah (Mk 9:5), or when he denied Christ (Mk 14:66-72). Even after Pentecost, Peter was not totally preserved from personal weakness (Gal 2:11-14).

The same is true of the popes. Even though Catholics believe that God sometimes uses them to speak a sure word of truth to the church, this does not mean that everything they say is infallible. In fact, the Catholic Church has established some rigorous conditions to determine what can be considered an infallible statement of a pope. The First Vatican Council (1869-70) was the first ecumenical council to formally define what Catholics believe about the infallibility of the pope, even though Catholic Christians had recognized his special teaching authority for many centuries. (The Catholic Church often does not formulate an official definition of its beliefs until these beliefs are questioned or require clarification.) Vatican I taught that in order for a statement of a pope to be considered "infallible," it must meet the following conditions:

1. The pope must be speaking *ex cathedra,* that is, "from the chair" of Peter, which means in his position as chief teacher and shepherd of Catholic Christians.

2. The pope must clearly define the doctrine as being a truth of faith.

3. It must be a definition concerning "faith or morals."[17]

These requirements have many implications. One is that the pope cannot speak infallibly about science, politics, economics, etc., unless the issue involved is directly related to Christian faith or morals. Another implication is that the pope speaks infallibly only when he explicitly defines a doctrine as an "article of faith." This condition excludes most of the "ordinary" teaching of the pope, such as encyclical letters, apostolic exhortations, occasional speeches, and off-hand comments. The Second Vatican Council affirmed the teaching of the First when it stated that the pope's teaching is infallible only when as supreme shepherd and teacher of all the faithful, who confirms his brethren in their faith (cf. Lk 22:32), he proclaims by a definitive act some doctrine of faith or morals.[18]

According to this standard, only two of the pope's teachings in recent times have been considered infallible definitions of Christian faith: the doctrine of the Immaculate Conception of Mary (1854) and the Assumption of Mary into heaven (1950). These two doctrines will be discussed fully later in the book when we discuss Catholic beliefs about Mary. They were defined not because they are the most important doctrines of the Catholic faith (most of those had been determined long ago by ecumenical councils and other papal teachings), but because they were two doctrines that some Catholics were uncertain about. The popes believed that the Holy Spirit had given them and the church sufficient insight to formally define these beliefs as true.

Although Catholics consider very few of the pope's statements to be infallible, Catholics are expected to respect and obey *all* forms of the pope's teaching. The Second Vatican Council teaches that

> this religious submission of will and of mind must be shown in a special way to the authentic teaching authority of the Roman Pontiff, even when he is not speaking *ex cathedra*. That is, it must be shown in such a way that his supreme magisterium is acknowledged with reverence, the judgments made by him are sincerely adhered to, according to his manifest mind and will. His mind and will in the matter may be known chiefly either from the character of the documents (in which the teaching is presented), from his frequent repetition of the same doctrine, or from his manner of speaking.[19]

The charism of infallibility is a great gift to the church, whether it is expressed through the united teaching of the bishops, through the pope defining a doctrine under the anointing of the Holy Spirit, or through the *sensus fidelium*—the whole Christian people being led to a belief through the "sense of the faith."[20] Catholic Christians believe that God uses all these channels to fulfill his promise to preserve his people in the truth until he comes again to reveal all truth in its fullness.

A final word may be said about the honor that Catholics give to the pope. The Bible frequently exhorts Christians to honor and respect the elders of the Christian community (1 Thes 5:12-13; Rom 13:1; 2 Tm 2:2, 24-25), and this would certainly include the pope. But the pope is not God, and Catholics do not honor him as God. Catholics respect the pope as a human representative of Jesus Christ—a "vicar" of Christ Jesus. The pope is called "holy father" because he has a fatherly care for all of God's people, like a good shepherd (Jn 10), and because his ministry reflects in an imperfect yet real way the perfect love and care of God the Father for his people. Most of all, Catholics respect the pope because they believe that he has been given a special gift to proclaim and defend the Word of God, as it has come to us in the Bible and the authentic Christian tradition. Catholics believe that in so respecting the pope and other Christian leaders, they are honoring God, who has raised them up as leaders of his church.

Catholic Christians rejoice and bend in awe before God that he has shown his love by using imperfect human beings to transmit and proclaim his perfect truth, and to guide us to the Father through Jesus Christ and in the power of the Holy Spirit.

SIX

The Work of the Holy Spirit

A MONG MANY CHRISTIANS TODAY there is a renewed interest in the Holy Spirit and his work. Unfortunately, this has also led to some misunderstandings and divisions. Words such as "charismatic renewal," "neo-Pentecostal movement," and "baptism in the Holy Spirit" are foreign and unsettling to many Catholics, and to many Protestants as well. And yet, this charismatic or Pentecostal movement claims to be a work of God's Holy Spirit, and has shown considerable ecumenical promise in its ability to draw Christians together to worship and share their lives across denominational lines. At the same time, this movement also has given rise to new ecumenical problems and misunderstandings.

In light of this situation, I think it is important to investigate the current trend of interest in the Holy Spirit in light of the Catholic understanding of the Spirit and his work among Christians.

But there is a more important reason for paying attention to the Holy Spirit. The Holy Spirit brings life to everything that Christians do and believe, and reveals their true meaning. Without the Holy Spirit, prayer is no more than meditation on ultimate reality or just "navel-gazing," the sacraments are empty, meaningless rituals, church leaders are merely bureaucrats or moralists, the Bible is just another great literary work, and the Christian life is observing a set of rules or fulfilling certain ideals by one's own effort. Only with the Holy Spirit is it possible to understand what Christianity is all about. Through the Holy Spirit, the Bible is perceived as God's inspired word in human language, church leaders carry on the mission of Jesus Christ by his authority and commission, the Christian life is marked by God's guidance and empowering, and prayer and the sacraments become personal encounters with the living God. This is why the Holy Spirit is essential to the Christian life, as Catholics understand it.

A good place to begin is a statement of the Second Vatican Council concerning the Holy Spirit's work:

> When the work which the Father had given the Son to do on earth was accomplished, the Holy Spirit was sent on the day of Pentecost in order that He might forever sanctify the Church. All believers have access to the Father through Christ in the one Spirit (Eph 2:18). He is the Spirit of life, a fountain of water springing up to life eternal (Jn 4:14, 7:38-39). Through him the Father gives life to men who are dead from sin, till at last he revives in Christ even their mortal bodies (Rom 8:10-11).
>
> The Spirit dwells in the Church and in the hearts of the faithful as in a temple (1 Cor 3:16, 6;19). In them he prays and bears witness to the fact that they are adopted sons (Gal 4:6; Rom 8:15-16, 26). The Spirit guides the Church into the fullness of truth (Jn 16:13) and gives her a unity of fellowship and service. He furnishes and directs her with various gifts, both hierarchical and charismatic, and adorns her with the fruits of his grace (Eph 4:11-12; 1 Cor 12:4; Gal 5:22). By the power of the gospel, he makes the Church grow, perpetually renews her, and leads her to perfect union with her Spouse. The Spirit and the Bride both say to the Lord Jesus, "Come!" (Rv 22:17). Thus the Church shines forth as "a people made one with the unity of the Father, the Son and the Holy Spirit."[1]

We have previously discussed the work of the Holy Spirit in leading the church into the fullness of truth (Jn 16:13), which Catholics call the gift of infallibility. But what about the statement, "The Spirit dwells in the Church and in the hearts of the faithful as in a temple" (see 1 Cor 3:16, 6:19; Eph 2:21-23)? What does it mean that the Holy Spirit dwells in the church and in each Christian? How does the Spirit come to dwell there? What difference does his presence make? These questions can serve as a framework for our study of the Spirit and his work.

The Holy Spirit: God's Gift to Each Christian

The Holy Spirit is God's greatest gift to each Christian. "Do you not know that your body is a temple of the Holy Spirit within you, which you have received from God?" (1 Cor 6:19). Jesus said that it was good that he was to depart from his apostles because unless he departed, he could not send them his Holy Spirit, who would bless them, empower them, and lead them into the fullness of truth (Jn 16:7-16; Acts 1:8).

How does he come to dwell within us? The Catholic Church emphasizes that a person becomes a Christian and first receives the Holy Spirit through belief and baptism. Belief is essential for a mature Christian to receive the Spirit. The letter to the Ephesians teaches: "When you heard the good news of salvation, the word of truth, and believed in it, you were sealed with the Holy Spirit who has been promised" (Eph 1:13). Concerning baptism, the apostle Paul noted that ". . . by one Spirit we were all baptized into one body" (1 Cor 12:13), and "he [God] saved us through the baptism of a new birth and renewal by the Holy Spirit" (Ti 3:6). Paul rejoiced that Jesus had lavished the Holy Spirit upon each believer (Ti 3:7) as a "pledge" or "first-fruits" (2 Cor 5:5; Rom 8:23) of the eternal life we hope to receive when we appear before the judgment seat of Christ. For Paul, the Holy Spirit was so important that he could say: "If a man does not possess the Spirit of Christ, he does not belong to him" (Rom 8:9). A person who has not received the Holy Spirit is not yet a Christian.

Paul's teaching, then, implies that the Holy Spirit is normally first given to individuals through belief and water baptism. The Acts of the Apostles also particularly associates the sending of the Spirit with baptism. Peter, in his speech on Pentecost, exhorted those who believed in Jesus to: "Repent, and be baptized every one of you in the name of Jesus Christ for the forgiveness of your sins; and you shall receive the gift of the Holy Spirit" (Acts 2:38). The relationship between being baptized in water and receiving the Holy Spirit is also seen in Acts 8:37-39; 9:17-18, 10:44-48, 11:15-17, 19:1-7. Baptism and the sending of the Spirit are meant to be inseparable. Acts records that if a person were baptized and did not receive the *fullness* of the Holy Spirit, the apostles would pray and lay their hands on them, begging God to send his Holy Spirit in greater measure (Acts 8:14-17). The Catholic sacrament of confirmation originates from this practice. Other New Testament texts that show how baptism and the sending of the Spirit are related include Matthew 28:19; Ephesians 4:4-5; John 1:25-34; 3:5.

These Bible passages are the basis for the Catholic teaching that a person becomes a "temple of the Holy Spirit" (1 Cor 6:19) through water baptism. Water baptism is not the only time or way that the Holy Spirit comes to live in a person, but the New Testament indicates the importance of being "baptized into Christ" (Rom 6:3), and thus being "sealed with the Holy Spirit" (Eph 1:13).

Are Catholics "Born Again" or "Spirit-filled?"

Many Christians today say that a person must be "born again," "Spirit-filled," or "baptized in the Holy Spirit" in order to be saved. Catholics and other Christians often ask what the Catholic Church teaches about this because these terms do not originate in Catholic teaching and theology. The simple answer is that the Catholic Church basically affirms the reality and truth of what these phrases point to.

Let us first consider the term "born again." It comes from Jesus' words in John 3:15: "Truly, truly, I say to you unless one is born anew [or "born from above" or "born again"], he cannot see the Kingdom of God... Unless one is born of water and the Spirit he cannot enter the Kingdom of God." Catholics believe that they are first born again of water and the Holy Spirit when they receive the sacrament of baptism. Therefore, a person who has been validly baptized has been "born of water and the Spirit" and can attain salvation.

However, Catholics also believe that baptism only *begins* the work or mission of the Holy Spirit in the life of the believer. The Spirit also comes in new and deeper ways in the other sacraments of the church, and through the fervent and expectant prayer of Christians. Salvation, as we have seen, is a life-long process that depends upon continually living in the power of the Holy Spirit and by the Spirit's guidance. Catholics do not believe that it is enough to be "born again" once (say, in baptism) and depend upon that fact alone for salvation. Paul stresses that it is those who *live* according to the Spirit of God who will attain salvation, ". . . for if you live according to the flesh you will die, but if by the Spirit you put to death the deeds of the body you will live. For all who are led by the Spirit of God are sons of God" (Rom 8:13-14).

The Fruit of the Spirit

The Holy Spirit is the continual guide and source of strength for the moral life of a Christian. In his letter to the church in Galatia, the apostle Paul indicates that the mark of truly "born again" Christians is that they do not live according to "the flesh" (carnal desires that are opposed to God's will), but according to the Spirit: ". . . walk by the Spirit and do not gratify the desires of the flesh" (Gal 5:16). So as to avoid any confusion, Paul lists the "works of the flesh" that lead to death (Gal 5:19-21), and contrasts them with the "fruit of the Spirit" that leads to life:

> But the fruit of the Spirit is love, joy, peace, patience, kindness, goodness, faithfulness, gentleness, self-control. Against such there is no law, and those who belong to Christ Jesus have crucified the flesh with its passions and desires. If we live by the Spirit, let us also walk by the Spirit.
> (Gal 5:22-25)

Again, Paul stresses that Christians must persevere in "walking by the Spirit" to the end of our lives in order to be saved: "for he who sows to his own flesh will reap corruption, but he who sows to the Spirit will from the Spirit reap eternal life. And let us not grow weary in doing good, for in due season we shall reap, if we do not lose heart." (Gal 6:8-9).

Thus the person who is truly "born again" and "Spirit-filled" is not necessarily the one who has had an extraordinary experience of the Holy Spirit at some point (though this is a blessing), but the person who lives and "walks" by the Holy Spirit; who has put to death the "works of the flesh" and manifests the "fruit of the Spirit." This is what it means to be a "new creation" in Christ Jesus—"the old has passed away—behold, the new has come!" (2 Cor 5:17).

Catholic tradition has always emphasized that the Holy Spirit clearly manifests his presence in the life of the truly "born again" Christian through the fruit of the Spirit, and leads a person to salvation who continues to live by the Spirit until life's end.

"Baptized in the Holy Spirit"

Many Catholics today are claiming to be "baptized in the Holy Spirit," and are testifying to others that this has made a great difference in their lives. Because this is a potential source of controversy and misunderstanding among Catholics, not to mention among all Christians, we should determine what it means to be "baptized in the Holy Spirit," and inquire whether this conforms to true Catholic theology.

First, what does it mean to be "baptized in the Spirit?" The phrase itself is biblical. John the Baptist prophesied that Jesus "will baptize you with the Holy Spirit . . ." (Mt 3:11; Mk 1:8; Lk 3:16; Jn 1:33). In the account of Jesus' ascension to the Father in Acts, Jesus promised his disciples, "before many days you shall be baptized with the Holy Spirit" (Acts 1:5). The fulfillment of this prophecy began with the sending of the Holy Spirit upon the disciples at Pentecost.

Catholics have often associated being "baptized in the Holy Spirit" with water baptism, and we have seen that the Bible does relate the two. However, the Catholic Church has never claimed that the work of the Holy Spirit is limited exclusively to baptism. Again, the Bible, especially the Acts of the Apostles, implies that it may be necessary to pray that a baptized person receive a greater outpouring of the Holy Spirit. The Catholic understanding of the sacrament of confirmation affirms this. Confirmation is the Catholic Church's official prayer for the Holy Spirit to empower a person to spread the gospel, to live a fervent Christian life, and to share more fully in the mission and ministry of the church.

The Catholic Church also teaches that the Spirit of God can enter a person's life in a new way if the person simply prays for this with expectant faith. Sometimes, as in the case of Paul, God sends his Spirit to a person even without their prayer or faith. The receiving of the Holy Spirit in a new way, usually as a result of earnest, expectant prayer, is what many Christians today call being "baptized in the Holy Spirit." Nothing in official Catholic teaching denies the possibility or the importance of this. On the contrary, some of the greatest Catholic saints have urged Christians to continually ask God for a fuller outpouring of the Holy Spirit in their lives. The well-known Catholic prayer to the Holy Spirit implores God to send the Spirit to "fill the hearts of your faithful," to "enkindle in them the fire of your love," and to "renew the face of the earth." At the opening of the Second Vatican Council, Pope John XXIII called upon all Catholics to pray: "Renew your wonders in our time, as though by a new Pentecost . . ."[2] Both Pope Paul VI and Pope John Paul II have endorsed and warmly supported the various movements in the Catholic Church that have focused on the renewing work of the Holy Spirit in lives of Christians.[3]

In summary, although Catholics may not necessarily use the same terminology as other Christians, the Catholic Church proclaims the importance of the Holy Spirit in the life of each Christian and the church.

"Baptism in the Spirit" and Catholic Theology

Catholic theologians have reflected on the work of the Holy Spirit in our lives and have discussed some important questions about how "baptism in the Spirit" is related to other forms of God's action among his people. Some Catholic theologians have proposed other terms to describe this work of God: "renewal of the Spirit," "release of the Spirit," "new outpouring of the Spirit," and others. The reason for these proposals is to acknowledge that "baptized in the Spirit" is a biblical term which probably should not be used to describe one particular type of experience of the Holy Spirit. To speak of "*the* baptism in the Spirit" is even more misleading if it implies that there is only one event in a person's life that could be properly called by that name. God can pour out the Holy Spirit in a new and significant way many times in a person's life if he wishes. The first time that this happens to a person is often the most dramatic, because it may be experienced by the person as a totally "new thing." Thus people speak of "*the* baptism in the Spirit." But God certainly can and does pour out his Holy Spirit many times in a person's life, often in response to faith-filled prayer.

Theologians have also examined the relationship between being "baptized in the Holy Spirit" and the sacraments, especially baptism and confirmation. Some maintain that being "baptized in the Spirit" is actually a "release" or a "coming to consciousness," of the power of the Holy Spirit who already has been given fully to the believer through the sacraments of the church. Fr. Francis Sullivan, S.J., refers to St. Thomas Aquinas' teaching on the subject:

> The two key words which for St. Thomas express what happens when the Holy Spirit is given or sent to us are *inhabitation* and *innovation*, the Holy Spirit dwells in us, in such a way as to *make us new*.
>
> Now, of course, in Catholic teaching this takes place initially at the moment when we become Christians, when we are "born of water and the Spirit" (Jn 3:5). But St. Thomas also asks the question whether we can speak of a sending of the Spirit to a person in whom he is already indwelling, and if so, how this is to be understood.[4]

When asked whether we could speak of a *new* "sending" of the Holy Spirit to someone in whom the Spirit was already indwelling (through the sacraments, for example), St. Thomas replied:

> There is an invisible sending (of the Holy Spirit) also with respect to an advance in virtue or an increase of grace . . . Such an invisible sending is especially to be seen in that kind of increase of grace whereby a person moves forward into some new act or new state of grace: as, for instance, when a person moves forward into the grace of working miracles, or of prophecy, or out of the burning love of God offers his

life as a martyr, or renounces all of his possessions, or undertakes some other such arduous thing.[5]

After commenting on this passage, Fr. Sullivan states

> I conclude from this teaching of St. Thomas that there is no reason why Catholics, who believe that they have received the Holy Spirit in their sacramental initiation, should not look forward to new "sendings" of the Spirit to them, which would move them from the "state of grace" in which they already are into some "new act" or "new state of grace." Now if we recall that in biblical language, "sending the Spirit," "pouring out the Spirit," and "baptizing in the Spirit" are simply different ways of saying the same thing, the conclusion follows that it is quite in accord with traditional Catholic theology for baptized and confirmed Christians to ask the Lord to "baptize them in the Holy Spirit." What they are asking for, in the language of St. Thomas, is a new "sending" of the Holy Spirit, which would begin a decisively new work of grace in their lives. As we have seen from the examples which St. Thomas gives, (working miracles, prophecy, etc.) he would obviously not be surprised if such a new work of grace involved a charismatic gift.[6]

Fr. Sullivan goes on to explain that this new sending of the Holy Spirit is more than the conferral of a new gift (or gifts) of the Spirit, but "a new way of the Spirit's indwelling in the soul ... a real innovation (making new) of the person's relationship with the indwelling Spirit."[7] He also believes that it is incorrect to claim that a person has been "baptized in the Holy Spirit" if the person has no awareness of anything "new" in his relationship with God. Unlike the sacraments, in which Catholics believe that God unfailingly confers his grace, the prayer for the "baptism of the Holy Spirit" may or may not result in God conferring this gift. As Fr. Sullivan comments "if 'baptism in the Spirit' means coming into some new experience of the Spirit in one's life, then I do not see how a person can be said to have been 'baptized in the Spirit' in this sense, unless there is some kind of experienced change in that person's Christian life."[8]

Many Catholics today are becoming aware of their need for a deeper knowledge of God and are seeking a fuller release or outpouring of the power of the Holy Spirit in their lives. Many of these Catholics have been regularly receiving the sacraments and striving to live uprightly but they experience "something missing"—the desire and need for more of God and his Holy Spirit. Hence, they are right to pray to God and seek the prayers of others to be "baptized in the Holy Spirit." They open themselves to receive the full range of gifts (charisms) and other manifestations of the Holy Spirit. (Catholics do *not* believe, however, that any particular gift, such as "speaking in tongues" *always* and necessarily accompanies being "baptized in the Spirit." See 1 Cor 12:29-31; 14:5).

How the "Invisible" Spirit Is Revealed

For many Christians, the Holy Spirit is the "invisible" member of the Trinity. Certainly it is a biblical truth that the Holy Spirit's mission is not to exalt himself but to direct us to Jesus Christ and through him to the Father. It is also a fact that the Bible often portrays the Holy Spirit by elusive images such as breath or wind, living water, fire, and a dove, which makes it difficult for us to picture the Holy Spirit as a person—which he is. However difficult it may be to conceptualize the Holy Spirit with our minds, the Bible makes it evident that believers should know God's presence in their "hearts" by the Holy Spirit living within them. In his letter to the Romans, Paul says that "God's love has been poured into our hearts through the Holy Spirit who has been given us" (Rom 5:5), and that

when we cry, "Abba! Father" it is the Spirit himself bearing witness with our spirit that we are children of God. . . .

Likewise, the Spirit helps us in our weakness; for we do not know how to pray as we ought, but the Spirit himself intercedes for us with sighs too deep for words."

(Rom 8:15, 16, 26)

Paul also poses questions in his letters that presuppose that the Spirit is someone when Christians really experience in their lives. "Did you receive the Spirit by works of the law or by hearing with faith?" (Gal 3:2). "Does your life in Christ make you strong? Does his love comfort you? Do you have fellowship with the Holy Spirit?" (Phil 2:1, TEV).

Unfortunately, many Christians today, including many Catholic Christians, are unable to answer these questions confidently because they are not fully aware of the presence of the Holy Spirit in their lives. They are like the Christians at Ephesus whom when Paul asked, "Did you receive the Holy Spirit when you believed?" replied "No, we have never even heard that there is a Holy Spirit" (Acts 19:2).

Many Catholics and other Christians are praying to be "baptized in the Spirit" so that the Holy Spirit will become a living reality in their lives. In the Gospel of John, Jesus promised that the Holy Spirit would be like "rivers of living water" flowing from the heart of believers (Jn 7:37-39). The Acts of the Apostles records numerous instances in which the Holy Spirit entered the lives of believers in a new way, and testified to his presence in them by spiritual gifts, boldness in witnessing to Jesus Christ and his gospel, guidance for their lives, and even healings and miracles. All this is portrayed in the New Testament as the normal experience of Christians. Many Christians today (including Catholics) are re-discovering this normal Christian experience when they earnestly pray to God to send his Spirit into their lives in a new way and expect that he will do this. They pray to be "baptized in the Holy Spirit," and in this prayer open themselves to whatever gifts or manifestations of the Spirit that God wishes to give them. Christians expect that God will answer such a prayer because Jesus himself taught:

Ask and it will be given you, seek and you will find; knock and it will be opened to you. For everyone who asks receives, and he who seeks finds, and to him who knocks, it will be opened. What father among you, if his son asks for a fish, will instead of a fish give him a serpent; or if he asks for an egg, will give him a scorpion? If you then, who are evil, know how to give good gifts to your children, how much more will the heavenly Father give the Holy Spirit to those who ask him! (Lk 11:9-13)

Manifestations of the Holy Spirit's Presence

How can we discern whether the Holy Spirit is truly present, or has come in a new way if we ask him to come? The apostle Paul gives us a number of "indicators" that help us determine this.

First, in 1 Corinthians 12:3, Paul writes: "No one speaking by the Spirit of God ever says 'Jesus be cursed!' and no one can say 'Jesus is Lord' except by the Holy Spirit." The first sign of the Holy Spirit's presence is that he leads people to acknowledge that Jesus Christ is Lord, and to commit their lives to him.

The second sign, mentioned previously, is that the Holy Spirit empowers people to lead holy lives—to manifest the "fruit of the Spirit" and to put to death the "works of the flesh." "If we live by the Spirit, let us also walk by the Spirit" (Gal 5:25). Christians who are filled with the Spirit act in a way which befits one who has received the Spirit. "For God has not called us for uncleanness, but in holiness. Therefore, whoever disregards this, disregards not men but God, who gives his Holy Spirit to you" (1 Thes 4:7, 8). "For God did not give us a spirit of timidity but a spirit of power and love and self-control" (2 Tm 1:7). The Holy Spirit confers the power which makes it possible for Christians to be holy and to live in true freedom, according to God's will (Gal 5:1, 13-16). If a Christian's life does not manifest a greater holiness, "the fruit of the spirit," and freedom from sin, it is questionable whether the Holy Spirit has entered a person's life in a new way.

Thirdly, the Holy Spirit reveals his presence through the gifts he bestows on us. The Bible presents two lists of the gifts of the Holy Spirit. The book of the prophet Isaiah tells of the gifts which now are available to every follower of Jesus, the Messiah:

> The spirit of the Lord shall rest upon him: the spirit of wisdom and of understanding, the spirit of counsel and of fortitude, the spirit of knowledge and of piety. And he shall be filled with the spirit of the fear of the Lord. He shall not judge according to the sight of the eyes, nor reprove according to what he hears (Is 11:2-3).

These seven gifts—wisdom, understanding, counsel, fortitude, knowledge, piety, and fear of the Lord, have traditionally been recognized by Catholics as manifestations of the Holy Spirit's indwelling in the believer—"gifts" of the Holy Spirit.

But there is also another list of gifts of the Spirit in the Bible. The apostle Paul presents and explains them most fully in his first letter to the Corinthians. First he notes that only those who have received the Holy Spirit ("spiritual men") are able to understand these gifts—to others they are foolish.

> Now we have received not the spirit of the world, but the Spirit which is from God, that we might understand the gifts bestowed on us by God. And we impart this in words not taught by human wisdom but taught by the Spirit, interpreting spiritual truths to those who possess the Spirit.
>
> The unspiritual man does not receive the gifts of the Spirit of God, for they are folly to him, and he is not able to understand them because they are spiritually discerned.
> (1 Cor 2:12-14)

This explains why Christians who recognize the gifts of the Spirit in their own lives often have difficulty explaining them to others, even to other Christians who are not aware of the gifts of the Spirit in their lives.

The fact is that *every* Christian who has received the Holy Spirit has also received gifts of the Spirit, or charisms. Paul taught "to *each* is given the manifestation of the Spirit for the common good" (1 Cor 12:7). This is also the official teaching of the Catholic Church. Vatican II's "Dogmatic Constitution on the Church" states:

It is not only through the sacraments and Church ministries that the Holy Spirit sanctifies and leads the people of God and enriches it with virtues. Allotting His gifts "to everyone according as he wills" (1 Cor 12:11), He distributes special graces among the faithful of every rank. By these gifts He makes them fit and ready to undertake the various tasks and offices advantageous for the renewal and upbuilding of the Church, according to the words of the Apostles: "The manifestation of the Spirit is given to everyone for profit" (1 Cor 12:7). These charismatic gifts, whether they be the most outstanding or the more simple and widely diffused, are to be received with thanksgiving and consolation, for they are exceedingly suitable and useful for the needs of the Church.[9]

Some Catholics resist the title "charismatic," but the word simply means "gifted," or more precisely, "possessing gifts of the Holy Spirit." Both the Bible and the Second Vatican Council state that all Christians possess "charisms" or gifts of the Holy Spirit, and therefore it is correct to say that Christians (including Catholic Christians) are "charismatic." Hence, it can be misleading to use the word "charismatic" exclusively to designate a particular group or movement within the church. God wills *all* Christians to desire and receive the gifts of the Holy Spirit. St. Paul exhorted the Corinthians to "earnestly desire the spiritual gifts" (1 Cor 14:1). The Second Vatican Council, quoted above, insisted that "these charismatic gifts are to be received with thanksgiving and consolation, for they are exceedingly suitable and useful for the needs of the church."[10]

Catholics should pray that God will send his Holy Spirit, and the gifts of the Spirit, more abundantly to all his people. We should pray that we will no longer need "charismatic renewal," but will have a truly charismatic church in which every believer gladly receives the Holy Spirit and the gifts of the Spirit that God wishes to give, and uses these gifts for the upbuilding of God's people.

The Nature and Purpose of Spiritual Gifts

What are these "gifts of the Spirit" that are a sign of the Holy Spirit's presence in the believer? Besides the ones mentioned in the book of Isaiah, Paul lists some others in 1 Corinthians 12:8-10: word of wisdom, word of knowledge, faith, healing, working of miracles, prophecy, discernment of spirits, speaking in tongues and the interpretation of tongues. In 1 Corinthians 12:28 he lists ministries related to these gifts: apostles, prophets, teachers, miracle workers, healers, helpers, administrators, and speakers in tongues. Ephesians 4:11 lists apostles, prophets, evangelists, pastors, and teachers. Paul probably did not mean these lists to be complete or exhaustive, but representative of the wide variety of the Holy Spirit's gifts to believers.

Paul teaches that the main purpose of the gifts of the Spirit is to build up the church—the body of Christ. "To each is given the manifestation of the Spirit *for the common good*" (1 Cor 12:7). The gifts are "for the equipment of the saints, for the work of ministry, for building up the body of Christ" (Eph 4:11-12). In 1 Cor 12-14, Paul emphasizes that the gifts of the Holy Spirit are not given primarily for the individual's own spiritual growth, but for the good of the whole body of Christ. The more valuable gifts are those which build up the church, and not just the individual who possesses them (1 Cor 14:1-5) "so with yourselves, since you are eager for manifestations of the Spirit, strive to excel in building up the church" (1 Cor 14:12).

Paul insists that the key to using the gifts properly is to use them in love. In 1 Corinthians 13, he stresses that the gifts are useless unless they are used to love God and other people. He also points out that all of the gifts of the Spirit will pass away when Jesus Christ comes in glory. Only faith, hope, and love will last forever—"but the greatest of these is love" (1 Cor 13:8-13).

Catholics do not make a sharp distinction between the "hierarchy" of the church and "charismatic leaders." Those who hold positions of ordained leadership (the "hierarchy") *are* "charismatic leaders," because it has been discerned that God has given them the charisms or gifts necessary to lead God's people. They have been set aside for these ministries because they possess certain natural talents and gifts of the Holy Spirit that equip them to serve God's people as ordained leaders. The pastoral epistles, for example, list the human and spiritual gifts that qualify a person to serve as a bishop or deacon. The letter to the Ephesians affirms that being an apostle, prophet, evangelist, pastor or teacher is a gift of God (Eph 4:11). Thus, when the church's ordained ministers do not appear to be using their human and spiritual gifts fully, this does not necessarily mean that these are lacking. Who among us uses all of our gifts fully? The gifts of the Holy Spirit need to be nurtured and cultivated in order to be effective. This is true of both ordained ministers, and of every member of the church. Catholics must encourage both their ordained leaders and each other in their use of the gifts of the Holy Spirit so that these gifts will be more fruitful in the life of the church.

But the gifts of the Spirit are not limited to the church's "official" or ordained leaders. "To *each* is given the ma˚ ˚

tion of the Spirit for the common good" (1 Cor 12:7). *Every* Christian has a gift of the Holy Spirit for the strengthening of the Body of Christ. The Second Vatican Council emphasized that every Christian has a mission to spread the gospel of Jesus Christ and to build up the church. We are prepared and equipped for this mission through the gifts of the Holy Spirit. The Second Vatican Council taught:

> For the exercise of this apostolate, the Holy Spirit who sanctifies the People of God through the ministry and the sacraments gives to the faithful special gifts as well (cf. 1 Cor 12:7), "allotting to everyone according as he wills" (1 Cor 12:11). Thus may the individual, "according to the gift each has received administer it to one another" and become "good stewards of the manifold grace of God" (1 Pt 4:10), and build up thereby the whole body in charity (cf. Eph 4:16).
>
> From the reception of these charisms or gifts, including those which are less dramatic, there arises for each believer the right and duty to use them in the church and in the world for the good of mankind and for the upbuilding of the church. Believers, in so doing, need to enjoy the freedom of the Holy Spirit who "breathes where he wills" (Jn 3:8). At the same time, they must act in communion with their brothers in Christ, especially with their pastors. The latter (pastors) must make a judgment about the true nature and proper use of these gifts, not in order to extinguish the Spirit, but to test all things and hold fast to what is good (cf. 1 Thes 5:12, 19, 21).[11]

Although an examination of the social teaching of the Catholic Church is beyond the scope of this book, it is the Holy Spirit who guides Christians in their social concern and action and who provides the gifts that equip them to accomplish God's purposes in this area. Thus, all Catholic Christians have a right and a duty to use their gifts of the Holy

Spirit for the good of mankind and of the church. It is also important to note that while the use of these gifts requires a certain "freedom of the Holy Spirit," there is also a proper order for their use. Catholics must exercise these gifts "in communion with their brothers in Christ, especially with their pastors."[12]

An analogy that has helped me to understand how the gifts of the Spirit function in proper order is to compare the church with an orchestra. In an orchestra, each musician's instrument is important and has a part to play in producing a beautiful symphony. The conductor of the orchestra has the role of coordinating and directing all of the musicians' parts so that this effect is achieved. The same is true of the church. Each Christian has a gift of the Holy Spirit that is important to the church's mission and each Christian must use that gift if the church's mission is to be fully accomplished. The bishop, working with other ordained leaders, has the gift and the responsibility to coordinate and direct the overall work of the church, so that each Christian's unique gift and contribution blends in with all the others and builds up the body of Christ.

The fact that God uses his ministers to orchestrate the operation of the spiritual gifts is an example of the incarnational principle. God works through human beings to fulfill his plan and purposes. Note that this does not mean that apostles, bishops, and pastors are more important in God's plan. The conductor could not accomplish his task without the *whole* orchestra present to play. The apostles,' bishops' or pastors' role would be useless, or at least limited, if each Christian were not present in the church, each ready to exercise his or her own unique gift of the Spirit in accordance with God's direction, which is often shown through the guidance of the church's ordained leaders. Thus, the "charismatic" and the "hierarchical" dimensions of the church are not in conflict, but are complementary and united in their goal of serving the Lord and promoting the work of his kingdom.

SEVEN

The Sacraments

CHRISTIANS BELIEVE THAT JESUS, by the suffering and death
he freely underwent for our salvation, has poured out the
Holy Spirit and all of God's grace upon mankind. The cross of
Jesus is like a fountain, from which the "living water" of the
Holy Spirit and all the abundant streams of God's life and
blessings flow. All men and women can come there to drink
and find life. The sacraments are simply channels through
which the grace of God, flowing from the cross of Jesus,
comes to us. They are not the only channels of God's grace
through Jesus, but they are reliable channels that never run
dry.

The sacraments are not "magic." The power and life they
convey comes from God through Jesus Christ. Separated from
the cross of Jesus Christ and from his grace, the sacraments
would be only dry, barren ditches—empty, meaningless
rituals. But because they are inseparably linked to the life,
death, and resurrection of Jesus, the sacraments are full of
God's abundant life.

We receive the benefits of the grace and salvation that Jesus
won for us by simply coming to him. We must, "Come to him,
to that living stone, rejected by men but in God's sight chosen
and precious" (1 Pt 2:4). One way of coming to that living
stone, Jesus Christ, is through the sacraments. If we want to

taste the water running in a stream, we must stoop down and drink. To "drink" the graces and blessings of the sacraments we must come to them in faith that God's grace and power are available in these "living streams." Further, Catholics must not only bend down to the stream but must also open their mouths to drink! In other words, we must participate in the sacraments not merely externally, but with real faith and expectancy that God himself is present there and wishes to act in our lives through them.

The sacraments confer spiritual life and power only because they are channels of the life and power of Jesus Christ. The grace of Christ is not limited to the sacraments, but the sacraments make it available to us in a unique and reliable way. The sacraments, then, are an abundant source of God's grace for all those who come to them with faith, desiring to grow closer to God through Jesus Christ.

The Incarnational Principle

Catholic Christians believe that the grace of Jesus Christ is present in the sacraments because the Bible, the activity of the apostles, and the tradition of the early church all testify to this belief. The sacraments are a prime example of God's "incarnational" way of approaching and relating to mankind. This means that God doesn't only share his life with us in an invisible or "spiritual" way, but also through things, persons, and events that we can touch and experience with our senses.

The Catholic Church teaches that the first and primary sacrament is Jesus Christ himself. God chose to save mankind and communicate the fullness of his life and grace by becoming a *man* who lived and walked among us. The first letter of John begins:

That which was from the beginning, which we have heard, which we have seen with our eyes, which we have looked upon and touched with our hands, concerning the word of life—the life was made manifest and we saw it and testify to it, and proclaim to you the eternal life which was with the Father and was made manifest to us (1 Jn 1:1-2).

Who would have guessed that the infinite God would reveal himself to us in a way that we could actually see and touch? Yet this is exactly what God did through the Word of Life, Jesus Christ, who is "Emmanuel," that is, "God with us" (Mt 1:23).

When "the Word became flesh and lived among us" (Jn 1:14), God began a new way of relating to mankind. In Jesus, God came down to our level and presented himself directly to all of our senses. Another way of saying this is that Jesus himself was the first "sacrament" of God.

Catholics believe that there are other "sacraments." Why? Essentially because Jesus himself established certain ways or "channels" of sharing his life and power with mankind. The Gospels record that Jesus sent out the Twelve and others of his followers (e.g., the "seventy-two" in Luke's gospel) with the same power and authority that he possessed. In fact, Jesus even boldly promised his disciples, "the man who has faith in me will do the works I . . . do, and greater far more than these" (Jn 14:12). In other words, Jesus used certain *people* as visible human channels of the same grace that was at work in him. Catholics believe that Jesus meant all his followers, the whole church, to be a sacrament of God's grace to the world—a channel by which his grace and power would enter the world even after he had departed. Therefore, the church of Jesus Christ rightly may be called a sacrament. The Catholic bishops at the Second Vatican Council taught about this understanding of the church as a sacrament in the "Dogmatic Constitution on the Church":

> By her relationship with Christ, the Church is a kind of sacrament of intimate union with God, and of the unity of all mankind, that is, she is a *sign* and *instrument* of such union and unity. . . .[1]

Christ ... through his Spirit, has established his body, the Church, as the universal sacrament of salvation. Sitting at the right hand of the Father, He is continually active in the world, leading men to the Church, and through her joining them more closely to Himself.[2]

So, although the church is not explicitly called a "sacrament" in the Bible, the church functions as a sacrament because it is a visible body that carries on the mission of Jesus Christ in the world and draws people to him. It is a channel, a sign, and an instrument of God's grace to all mankind.

Visible Signs

Besides using persons to carry on his mission and communicate the grace of God, Jesus also employed specific actions and objects as visible signs of the life and blessings he came to give. Water was one such sign, as when Jesus was baptized by John in the Jordan River and the Holy Spirit descended upon him (Mk 1:9-11). Jesus used ordinary food to show the power of God. His first miracle in John's gospel was to change water into wine (see Jn 2:1-11), and later he multiplied bread and fish to feed the hungry crowds (see Mk 6:35-44, 8:19). Jesus' actions and gestures communicated the grace and power of God. He often touched people when he healed them, even lepers (Mk 1:40-45), and used his own spit to open a blind man's eyes (see Mk 8:22-26). He breathed on the apostles to give them the Holy Spirit (Jn 20:22), and he gave them his own body and blood on the night before he died in the form of bread and wine (Mk 14:22-25). All of these are instances of Jesus' use of "sacraments"—specific objects, gestures, and persons that visibly symbolized and conferred God's abundant grace and blessings.

The sacraments recognized by the Catholic Church are all based upon some aspect of Jesus' life or teaching, even though he did not explicitly command his followers to carry out all of them after he departed. The sacraments emerged as a distinctive part of the church's life as the apostles followed Jesus' example or carried out his teaching. They anointed the sick for healing (see Mk 6:13). They laid their hands on people and prayed for them to receive the Holy Spirit (see Acts 8:14-17, 19:5-6). They laid their hands on others to be set apart for special ministry or mission in the church (see Acts 6:3-6, 13:1-3). They baptized (see Mt 28:19; Jn 4:2), and forgave sins with authority as Jesus had instructed and empowered them to do (see Mt 18:18; Jn 20:23). They came to understand marriage as a sacrament (which literally means "mystery"), representing the mystery of Jesus' love for the church (see Eph 5:21-33). And, of course, they offered bread and wine in thanksgiving ("eucharist") for Jesus' death, fulfilling his command to "do this in remembrance of me" (Lk 22:19).

The apostles knew that they were not Jesus, but they knew that Jesus himself was the one who was present with them and through them when they did those things in his name. As the Second Vatican Council said: "He [Jesus] is present in the sacraments by his power, in such a way that when someone baptizes, Jesus himself baptizes."[3] The sacraments and their human ministers are only channels of the grace and power of Jesus Christ.

The term "sacrament" was used more loosely in the early church than it is today. The Church Fathers of the first six centuries used the Latin word *sacramentum* and the synonymous Greek word *mysterion* to speak of many aspects of church life. In the Middle Ages, "sacrament" came to have a more precise meaning, and it became necessary to determine which of the church's ancient practices fit the more precise definition. By the thirteenth century, the bishops had agreed on an official list of the seven sacraments which Catholics and Orthodox Christians recognize today.

Although it took time for the church's formal understanding of sacraments to develop, the actual practice of these sacraments was a vital part of Christian life and worship from the first century on. We can now examine each of these sacraments more closely.

Baptism

The Bible emphasizes the importance of baptism in receiving God's gift of salvation:

> He saved us, not on the basis of deeds which we have done in righteousness, but according to his mercy, by the washing of regeneration [baptism] and renewing by the Holy Spirit.
>
> (Ti 3:5)

> Jesus answered, "Truly, truly I say to you, unless one is born of water and the Spirit, he cannot enter the Kingdom of God." (Jn 3:5)

> ... When the patience of God kept waiting in the days of Noah, during the construction of the ark, in which a few, that is eight persons were brought safely through the water, and corresponding to that, baptism now saves you.
>
> (1 Pt 3:20, 21)

Catholic Christians, therefore, view baptism as normally the first step in accepting God's salvation. Jesus himself commanded his apostles in his final appearance to them in Matthew's gospel. "Go therefore, and make disciples of all nations, baptizing them in the name of the Father, Son, and Holy Spirit" (Mt 28:19). The apostles began to fulfill this commission at Pentecost, when Peter exhorted the crowd to "repent, and be baptized everyone of you in the name of Jesus Christ for the forgiveness of your sins; and you shall receive the gift of the Holy Spirit" (Acts 2:38). Other passages in the Acts of the Apostles emphasize that baptism was the first step in becoming a Christian in the early church (see Acts

8:12-13, 8:37-38, 9:18, 10:47, 16:15, 19:5).

Two effects of baptism that Peter mentioned are the forgiveness of sins and reception of the Holy Spirit. Also, the baptized person enters into the fellowship of the body of Christ, the church (see Acts 2:41-42). As the apostle Paul explained, "for just as the body is one and has many members, and all the members of the body, though many, are one body, so it is with Christ. *For by one Spirit we were all baptized into one body* . . . and all were made to drink of one Spirit" (1 Cor 12:12-13). Paul also compared baptism with being buried with Christ, a burial that results in death to sin and the "old nature," and resurrection to life in God and the putting on of a completely new nature. As Paul wrote:

> Are you not aware that we who were baptized into Christ Jesus were baptized into his death? Through baptism into his death we were buried with him, so that just as Christ was raised from the dead by the glory of the Father, we too might live a new life. . . . His death was death to sin, once for all; his life is life for God. In the same way, you must consider yourselves dead to sin but alive for God in Christ Jesus. (Rom 6:1-4, 10-11)

> In baptism you were not only buried with him but also raised to life with him because you believed in the power of God who raised him from the dead (Col 2:12).

The early Christians symbolized this dying with Christ in baptism by fully immersing people in water three times, to signify Jesus' three days in the tomb. After that, the newly baptized persons were immediately clothed in white robes, symbolizing the "new creation" in Jesus (2 Cor 5:17) and then they were led into the assembly of the believers as new, full-fledged members of the church. They experienced the "first-fruits" of their salvation through the Holy Spirit entering their lives in baptism.

Infant Baptism

Who is eligible for baptism? The first converts to Christianity were adults. The New Testament does not explicitly state whether infants or children were also baptized, but there is some indication that they were. Immediately after Peter urged his hearers to be baptized in Acts 2, he explained: "For the promise is for you *and your children,* and for all who are far off, as many as the Lord our God shall call to Himself" (Acts 2:39). The New Testament also speaks of the baptism of "whole households" (1 Cor 1:16; Acts 10:48a; 16:15, 31, 33; 18:8), which in the normal Greek usage would include children. Paul drew a parallel between baptism and circumcision, which was normally administered to children (Col 2:11-12), and reminded the Corinthians that just as *all* the Jewish people (including children) were "baptized into Moses" by passing through the Red Sea, they were actually being blessed by Christ, the "spiritual rock that was following them" (1 Cor 10:4).

Perhaps the most thought-provoking New Testament text that could be applied to the baptism of infants and children is Jesus' teaching on the children who were brought to him for his blessing:

> People were bringing their little children to him to have him touch them, but the disciples were scolding them for this. Jesus became indignant when he noticed it and said to them: "Let the children come to me and do not hinder them. It is to such as these that the kingdom of God belongs. I assure you that whoever does not accept the reign of God like a little child shall not take part in it." Then he embraced them and blessed them, placing his hands on them.
>
> (Mk 10:13-16)

The fact that Jesus did not refuse to bless children and taught that the kingdom of heaven belongs to them influenced the Catholic Church in its decision to baptize infants and children.

In summary, the Bible does not explicitly command that infants and children be baptized, but neither does it forbid this practice. There is some scriptural support for the belief that that baptism is a blessing that Jesus wishes to confer on everyone, including children and infants.

There is no conclusive evidence before the third century that infants were baptized in the early church. After this, however, there is considerable evidence that infants and children were baptized, and by the fifth century this was a universally accepted practice throughout the church of Jesus Christ.

During the first few centuries of Christianity, not one important church leader, nor even any major heretical group, denied the validity of infant baptism. Some of them preferred to delay baptism because of the danger of falling into serious sin after receiving the sacrament, but they did not deny that infant baptism was valid. Many outstanding leaders of the early church testify, either directly or indirectly, to the church's practice of infant baptism. These leaders include Polycarp of Smyrna (167/8 A.D.), Justin Martyr (died c. 165 A.D.), Cyprian of Carthage (c. 249 A.D.), Irenaeus of Lyons (120-202 A.D.), Origen (185-254 A.D.), Hippolytus of Rome (170-236 A.D.), and others. St. Augustine explained the importance of baptizing infants for the remission (forgiveness) of original sin. Apparently, the Holy Spirit led Christians to baptize their children because they desired their salvation.

Since infant baptism is not universally practiced among Christians today, let us examine the Catholic Church's teaching on this matter in more detail. Children cannot have a mature understanding of the gospel and therefore cannot make a mature act of faith. The most common question about infant baptism is, "How can a parent or guardian's faith substitute for the faith of the child?"

It is noteworthy that Jesus did not pose this question. When

Jairus asked Jesus to raise his young daughter from the dead (Mk 5:22-23; 35-43) or another father asked Jesus to expel a demon from his son (Mk 9:17-27), Jesus acted with power because of *their* faith, not the faith of their children. How much more would Jesus desire to free children from an even worse bondage, the bondage of sin and eternal death, in response to the faith of their parents and of the whole Christian community? The Catholic Church believes that Jesus does respond in this way when infants and children are baptized.

But the Catholic Church also teaches that the parents of the baptized child must commit themselves to providing an environment for the child to grow in faith. This will prepare the child to make a personal faith commitment to Jesus Christ upon reaching maturity. This personal faith commitment is absolutely necessary for the mature Christian. One way that the Catholic Church stresses the necessity of this personal commitment to the Lord is by calling upon each person to renew their baptismal covenant each year at the Easter liturgy.

Finally, Catholics believe that infant baptism underscores the fact that salvation is a free gift of God. When someone baptizes, it is Christ who baptizes. He is the one who saves. Infant baptism reminds us that this salvation through baptism is not something the person could have earned or merited. It reminds us that the sacraments are primarily works of God, not of man, and that his initiative in our lives is most important. The infant did not choose to be baptized, but neither did he or she choose to be born. They are both God's gift, brought about through human agents: the child's parents. Just as the parents do their part in God's plan by initiating the child's physical life, they also can cooperate with God, through their faith, in initiating the child's eternal, spiritual life by presenting the child to be baptized.

For a similar reason, Catholic Christians do not accept the practice of "re-baptism." "Re-baptism" implies that God's work of salvation through baptism was ineffective the first time. Baptized children may turn away from God and choose to reject the grace of their baptism when they grow up, but if they turn back to God they have no need to be baptized again. They should simply repent and recommit themselves to following Jesus Christ, and ask God to renew and refresh in them the grace that they first received through baptism. The "prodigal son" left his family, sinned, and squandered his father's money, but he was welcomed back as a member of the family, not as an outsider. In the same way, a baptized Christian who goes astray remains a member of God's family through baptism, and need only turn away from sin and return to the family to be accepted back with full family status.

The Eucharist or the Lord's Supper

The word "eucharist" means "thanksgiving." This was the common name in the early church for the re-enactment of Jesus' last supper with his apostles. The essence of the Eucharist is the re-enactment of Jesus' action of distributing the bread and wine with the words, "Take, this is my body" (Mk 14:22); "This is my blood" (Mk 14:24); "Do this in remembrance of me" (Lk 22:19).

How are these words of Jesus to be understood? In the New Testament, the Greek word *estin* that is used in Jesus' saying, "This is my body," could mean either "is really" or "is figuratively" (or "signifies"). Both senses of the word occur in the New Testament. Which is correct? Is Jesus saying that the bread is *really* his body, and the wine is *really* his blood, or do they *symbolize* his body and blood?

Catholic Christians understand Jesus' words in light of the "commentary" on these words given in the Gospel of John and in Paul's letters, and in light of the testimony of the early Christians. Chapter 6 of John's Gospel, the last gospel written, implies that the early Christians had insisted that the eucharistic bread and wine were truly the body and blood of

Jesus, and that this had become a source of scandal to the Jews and others who were considering becoming Christians. John emphasizes that Jesus really meant that he expected his followers to eat his flesh and drink his blood (Jn 6:51-57), and that he predicted that many people would be scandalized and fall away from following him because of this teaching (Jn 6:60-64). When Jesus said, "unless you eat the flesh of the Son of man and drink his blood, you have no life in you" (Jn 6:53), he was speaking about them receiving his body and blood in the bread and wine of the Lord's supper or eucharist. This was no "symbolic" reception, according to John, but was actually eating the real body of Christ and drinking his real blood. This teaching is as much of a challenge to the faith of Christians today as it was to the readers of John's gospel. Catholic Christians accept this challenging teaching at its face value, and believe that when they receive the bread and wine of the Eucharist, they are actually partaking in the body and blood of Jesus Christ.

This understanding is also affirmed by the apostle Paul, who wrote in his first letter to the Corinthians: "The cup of blessing which we bless, is it not a participation in the blood of Christ? The bread which we break, is it not a participation in the body of Christ? Because there is one bread, we who are many are one body, for we all partake in the one bread" (1 Cor 10:16-17). Further on in this letter, after the re-stating Jesus' "words of institution," Paul concludes: "whoever, therefore, eats the bread or drinks the cup of the Lord in an unworthy manner will be guilty of profaning the body and blood of the Lord. Let a man examine himself, and so eat of the bread and drink of the cup. For anyone who eats and drinks without discerning the body eats and drinks judgment upon himself" (1 Cor 11:27-29). The most straightforward interpretation of these passages is that Paul considered the eucharistic bread and wine to be literally the body and blood of Christ.

How did the early Christians understand the Bible's teaching about the bread and wine of the Lord's Supper? To summarize a vast amount of literature, nearly every notable writing of the early church that mentions the Eucharist either implies or directly states that the bread and wine of the Lord's Supper is truly the body and blood of Jesus Christ. These include the writings of Ignatius of Antioch (c. 110 A.D., *Letter to the Smyrneans,* 7:1), Justin Martyr (c. 150 A.D., *First Apology,* Ch. 66), Irenaeus of Lyon (c. 185 A.D., *Against Heresies, Book V,* Ch. 2), Cyril of Jerusalem (c. 250 A.D., *Mystagogical Catecheses,* "Fourth Address: On the Body and Blood of Christ"), St. Augustine (c. 400 A.D., Sermon 272), and many others. I can find no reliable early Christian writer who did not believe that the bread and wine of the Eucharist is the body and blood of Christ. Hence, the Catholic understanding of the Eucharist as truly the body and blood of Christ is supported by both the New Testament and primitive Christian church.

Thus, Catholics speak of the "real presence" of Jesus Christ in the bread and wine of the Eucharist. If they are his body and blood, Jesus is "really present" there. This presence of Jesus can only be accepted in faith, since the outward appearance of the bread and wine does not change. Medieval Catholic theologians used the term "transubstantiation" to describe the mystery that the inner reality ("essence") of the bread and wine is transformed into the body and blood of Jesus, while the outward appearance ("accidents") remains the same. This doctrine is not intended to explain *how* this happens, or to reduce this mystery of faith to magic. It simply affirms, in faith, that Jesus' words are literally true: the bread and wine offered to God in the Eucharist become his body and blood. This explains why Catholic Christians have great reverence for the eucharistic bread and wine, since they believe that the Word of God is present in them just as fully as he was present in the physical body of Jesus. Catholics do not "worship the host," but worship Jesus Christ whom they discern by faith to be present in the host.

Should it surprise us that Jesus' body and blood are present in the eucharistic bread and wine? We believe that the fullness of God can take the form of a mere man—Jesus. Why should it be more difficult to believe (at Jesus' word) that God can be fully present in another part of his creation—bread and wine? If God submitted to be crucified for our salvation, is it any harder to believe that God would allow us to receive him into our bodies and spirits through a very basic human act, eating? The miracle of God's presence in the bread and wine of the Eucharist is comparable to the miracle of his presence among us in Jesus Christ. They are both beyond our comprehension, and reveal to us the depth of his love and his humility in placing himself at the disposal of his creatures, for the sake of our salvation.

The Mass

Because Jesus commanded his apostles to "do this in remembrance of me" (1 Cor 11:24; Lk 22:19), the Eucharist soon became the primary act of Christian worship in the primitive church. This re-enactment of the Lord's Last Supper was accompanied by readings from the Hebrew scriptures, accounts of Jesus' life and teaching, and prayers. Many early Christian writings record these various readings and prayers. This "prayer service," with the Eucharist as its center, came to be called "the Mass" by Catholics. Although the Mass has developed somewhat over the centuries, its parts are essentially the same as the worship services of the early church.

The weekly celebration of the Lord's Supper or the Eucharist was held on Sunday, the day of Jesus' resurrection. In the early church, it was generally assumed that all Christians who were physically able would gather every Sunday to worship the Lord and partake of his body and blood. The letter to the Hebrews warns against, "neglecting to meet together, as is the habit of some" (Heb 10:25). The Catholic Church today follows this practice in requiring its members to worship together on Sunday as a community. This is something that a faithful follower of Jesus and member of his body, the church, should desire to do, anyway.

It is not clear from the Bible who presided over the Eucharist or Lord's Supper. By the early second century, however, Ignatius of Antioch reported that only the bishop or his appointed representatives could lead the community in this sacrament: "You should all follow the bishop as Jesus did the Father. . . . You should regard that Eucharist as valid which is celebrated either by the bishop or someone he authorizes. Where the bishop is present, there let the congregation gather, just as where Jesus Christ is, there is the Catholic Church . . ."[5] This became the accepted pattern in the early church and beyond. Bishops became the primary leaders of the offical worship of the Christian community; they appointed presbyters or priests to assist them when their "flocks" ("dioceses") became too large for one man's sacramental ministry. The Catholic Church carries on this ancient practice of having only bishops and the presbyter/priests they appoint preside over the Eucharist. This makes biblical sense since only the apostles were given the direct commission by Jesus to "do this in remembrance of me," and the bishops are the ones who succeeded to the apostles' ministry and leadership.

The Mass As Sacrifice

Catholic Christians consider the second part of the Mass, the Liturgy of the Eucharist, as a representation or perpetuation of Jesus' one sacrifice of himself on Calvary for mankind's sins. However, the term "sacrifice of the Mass" is confusing and even scandalous to many Christians. The letter to the Hebrews states clearly that Jesus Christ has been sacrificed *once* for our sins, and now stands interceding for us in the presence of the Father (Heb 7:25, 9:24-28).

The Catholic Church has never taught that in the Mass Jesus is "re-sacrificed" or offered up to suffer again. The

Catholic Mass is called a sacrifice because it "re-presents," "re-enacts," or presents once again before us, the one sacrifice of Christ on Calvary. Jesus Christ was sacrificed once, but God, in his mercy, makes present to us once again the one sacrifice of Christ through the Mass so that we human beings can enter more deeply into the reality and significance of that sacrifice. Catholics believe that this is possible because Jesus Christ is "the same yesterday, today and forever" (Heb 13:8). What Jesus did in the *past*—his death on the cross—is *present* to God. God can make this sacrifice present to us when Christians gather to celebrate the Lord's Supper or Eucharist in his memory. Therefore, Catholic Christians believe that Jesus is not "re-sacrificed" in the Mass, but that his one sacrifice on Calvary is made real and present to us by God, so that we can enter into this central mystery of our faith in a new way. As the apostle Paul said, "For as often as you eat this bread and drink this cup, you proclaim the Lord's death until he comes" (1 Cor 11:26).⁶

Finally, a word should be said about the roles of the priest and the participants in the Mass. Catholic Christians affirm that Jesus made his whole people of the New Covenant "a kingdom of priests to God, his Father" (Rv 1:6 cf. 5:9-10); and "a royal priesthood" (1 Pt 2:9). This title can be applied to every Christian who participates in the prayer which is the Eucharist. The Second Vatican Council states: "The faithful, indeed, by virtue of their royal priesthood, participate in the offering of the Eucharist."⁷ How? At Mass, each Catholic is called to present his or her own life to God as a "living sacrifice" (Rom 12:1), by uniting it with the perfect, once-for-all sacrifice of Jesus Christ. Indeed, participation at Mass is not some magic rite in which the passive presence of an individual is adequate. In fact, the Roman Catholic code of canon law states that the eucharistic celebration should be "planned to bring about conscious, active, and full participation of the people, motivated by faith, hope, and charity."

Intercommunion

The Eucharist was intended by God to be a visible sign of the unity of his people in Jesus Christ. The apostle Paul wrote: "The bread which we break, is it not a participation in the body of Christ? Because there is one bread, we who are many are one body, for we all partake of the one bread." (1 Cor 10:16-17)

Today, the tragic reality is that the body of Christ is not one; it is divided into many churches and groups who disagree on many important issues. One of the issues that divides Christians is whether the bread and wine offered at the Eucharist or Lord's Supper truly becomes the body and blood of Christ. Christians also disagree about who has the proper authority to preside at the eucharistic celebration.

Catholic Christians consider these divisions and disagreements so serious that, except in special circumstances approved by the local bishop, they cannot in good conscience participate in communion services in other Christian churches, nor allow other Christians to receive the Eucharist in the Catholic Church, until these differences are resolved. Catholics believe that in the Eucharist they are truly receiving the body and blood of Jesus Christ in the outward form or "signs" of bread and wine. For Catholics, the reception of the Eucharist also expresses their communion or unity with the whole Catholic Church and its elders. Catholics believe that these elders, the bishops and the priests they ordain, preside over the eucharistic celebration through the authority they have received from Jesus Christ. This authority, as we have seen, has been passed on over the centuries through the bishops who have succeeded the apostles in leadership of God's people.

Catholics cannot in good conscience join with other Christians in this "sacrament of unity" while there still remains a basic disunity and disagreement with them about the

Eucharist itself, and about these other important points of Christian faith. Catholics understand participation in the Eucharist primarily as the ultimate sign of the unity that exists among Christians, rather than as a means for achieving unity. Catholic Christians realize that other Christians do not share this perspective, and so ask fellow Christians to abide by the Catholic understanding of intercommunion when they attend a Catholic service, just as Catholics wish to respect the beliefs of those who have a different point of view.

Jesus said, "If you bring your gift to the altar and there recall that your brother has anything against you, leave your gift at the altar, go first to be reconciled with your brother, and then come and offer your gift" (Mt 5:23-24). Catholics earnestly wish to seek reconciliation with other Christians, both as individuals and churches, so that we will be able to approach the altar of God together in genuine unity of mind and heart, belief and spirit. Until the day when the Lord heals the present disunity, the pain of the divisions that prevent Catholics from sharing the Lord's Supper with other Christians serves as a strong motivation for Catholics to pray and work for the unity of God's people.

The Eucharist: The Prayer of the Church

Because the Eucharist or the Lord's Supper makes present the central mystery of the Christian faith—the passion, death and resurrection of the Lord Jesus—Catholics consider it the highest form of Christian prayer. (This is not to exclude the "Our Father" which is an important part of the Mass). It is not just the prayer of the individual, nor of the priest who presides over it, but it is truly the prayer of the whole church, gathered to worship Jesus, our Savior and Great high priest (Heb 7:26, 27; 8:1).

The Second Vatican Council's "Constitution on the Sacred Liturgy" affirms this when it says that: "the liturgy (the Mass) is the summit toward which the activity of the Church is directed; at the same time it is the fountain from which all her power flows. For the goal of apostolic works is that all who are made sons of God by faith and baptism should come together to praise God in the midst of his church, to take part in her sacrifice and to eat the Lord's Supper."[8]

All the power of the church flows from the death and resurrection of Jesus Christ. All the church's many activities are brought together and offered to God as a sacrifice of praise in the liturgy of the Mass. The Mass reminds Catholics that all gifts and power in the church come from God and that the purpose of our lives is to worship God, to be nourished by God, and to offer all that we do back to him as a pleasing sacrifice by uniting it with the one truly acceptable sacrifice, the sacrifice of Jesus Christ.

The Second Vatican Council insisted that it is not enough for Catholics to participate in the liturgy in a merely external way:

> Before men can come to the liturgy they must be called to faith and conversion: "How then are they to call upon him in whom they have not believed?" (Rom 1:14). . . , In order that the sacred liturgy may produce its full effect, it is necessary that the faithful come to it with proper dispositions, that their thoughts match their words, and they cooperate with divine grace lest they receive it in vain. (Cf. 2 Cor 6:1)[9]

Where Catholics are participating in the liturgy of the Mass without true faith, conversion, or without the proper attitude of heart, they first must be called to repentance, faith, and conversion so that they will be worshipping not only in body, but "in Spirit and truth" (Jn 4:24).

The Sacrament of Reconciliation or Penance

Jesus scandalized many people by claiming to have the authority to forgive sins. "Why does this man speak thus? It is blasphemy! Who can forgive sins but God alone?" (Mk 2:7; Lk 7:49). But Jesus had the authority as the Son of God to forgive sins, and he gave this same authority to his apostles. To Peter he said, "Whatever you bind on earth shall be bound in heaven, and whatever you loose on earth shall be loosed in heaven" (Mt 16:18, 19). Later he told the other apostles the same thing (Mt 18:18). Even more directly, in John's gospel, Jesus appeared to the apostles on Easter and said, "Receive the Holy Spirit. If you forgive the sins of any, they are forgiven; if you retain the sins of any, they are retained" (Jn 20:22-23).

This follows a pattern that is consistent in the gospel. Jesus had special authority from his Father to establish the reign (or kingdom) of God on earth, and Jesus passed on this authority to his apostles so that they could continue his mission and ministry after he departed. He gave them the Holy Spirit as the source of their authority to forgive sins in Jesus' name. It is true that Jesus commanded *all* of his followers to forgive one another when someone sinned against them (Mt 6:14; Mt 18:21-22; Lk 17:3-4). But Jesus also gave his apostles a special authority to "bind and loose," or to forgive anyone's sins in God's name.

Again, following the pattern we have seen before, the apostles passed on their authority to forgive sins to the bishops. In the early church, formal forgiveness for sin, or absolution, was reserved for those who had committed very serious sins (such as murder, adultery, and apostasy), and it was accompanied by a long period of severe public penance.[10] A person could normally receive absolution for these sins only once in a lifetime; if he sinned seriously again, he could be readmitted to the church only as a public penitent. The early Christians took seriously the teaching of Paul about becoming a "new creation" when you were baptized. It was expected that a baptized person had the grace to avoid serious sin.

Because the formal forgiveness of serious sin in the church was restricted and involved severe penances, many converts to

Christianity began to delay being baptized until late in their lives. They feared falling into serious sin after baptism, and the rigors of public penance. A change in the understanding of this sacrament took place in the sixth and seventh centuries. Christian monks, probably in the context of spiritual direction, developed the practice of forgiving sins in Jesus' name as part of a more frequent private confession that included less serious sins. This eventually became the standard form of the sacrament.[11]

Some questions about the sacrament of reconciliation frequently arise. One is, simply, why is this sacrament necessary? Why not confess your sins directly to God? Why go to a priest, or any human being?

Certainly it is appropriate and even necessary to repent directly before God for one's sins. In fact, when Catholics participate in this sacrament they are primarily expressing their repentance and sorrow for sin to God, and seeking to be reconciled to him. However, Catholics believe that Jesus had a purpose in granting particular persons the authority to forgive sins in God's name. First, it is another aspect of God's "incarnational" way of relating to mankind; using human beings to continue his work on earth is part of the way God works. When our sins are forgiven by one who has been set apart by the church to represent Jesus Christ, we can experience the mercy of Jesus himself through that person.

Secondly, confessing sins to a person reminds one of the social dimension of sin. When someone sins, he not only offends God, but his sin also has an effect, either direct or indirect, on other people. The priest who grants God's forgiveness not only represents Jesus Christ, but also the whole Christian community, the church. Hence, the priest has the authority to reconcile a sinner to the body of Christ, the church.

Thirdly, the priest or minister is often able to counsel and encourage the penitent, or even pray with the penitent for healing of some area of sin or brokenness in the person's life. Jesus often uses his representative, the priest, to minister to the needs of people in remarkable ways through the sacrament of reconciliation.

Confirmation

Confirmation is the official prayer of the church for the full outpouring of the Holy Spirit in the life of a baptized Christian. Some aspects of the Catholic understanding of the sacrament of confirmation have already been discussed in the chapter on the Holy Spirit, but a brief summary will be presented here.

The Holy Spirit first comes to a person in baptism (see Acts 2:38), but the Acts of the Apostles also speak of a prayer for the outpouring of the Holy Spirit with the outward sign of a "laying on of hands." Peter and John were sent to converts in Samaria "and prayed for them that they might receive the Holy Spirit; for it had not yet fallen on any of them, but they had only been baptized in the name of the Lord Jesus. Then they laid their hands on them and they received the Holy Spirit" (Acts 8:15-17). Later in Acts, Paul baptized some disciples in the name of the Lord Jesus, and then, "when Paul laid hands upon them, the Holy Spirit came on them, and they spoke with tongues and prophesied" (Acts 19:6). Some theologians think that the only reason why these people lacked the Holy Spirit was because they were not initially baptized "in the name of the Father and of the Son and of the Holy Spirit" (Mt 28:19) as Jesus instructs, but baptized only in the name of Jesus.

In any case, the early church came to recognize that there was a prayer for the sending of the Holy Spirit that was distinct from baptism. Christians often received the full "release" or outpouring of the Holy Spirit through the prayer and "laying on of hands" of the apostles or one of their successors. Later, an anointing with oil was also added to the sacrament. This is the way the sacrament of confirmation originated. The work of the Holy Spirit was "confirmed" and strengthened in the life of the baptized Christian. The sacrament, of course, is based on the life of Jesus, upon whom the Holy Spirit descended in the form of a dove when he began his public ministry (Mk 1:9-11), who breathed upon his apostles after his resurrection with the words, "receive the Holy Spirit . . ." (Jn 20:22), and who sent the Holy Spirit in power upon all the disciples at Pentecost (Acts 2).

In the early church, confirmation accompanied baptism for adults. In the case of infant baptism, it became the practice of the Western church to delay confirmation until the child was older. In the Eastern Orthodox churches, infants are confirmed at the same time they are baptized.

Through the sacrament of confirmation, the Holy Spirit empowers God's people to proclaim the Good News of Jesus Christ, to live that message, and to continue Jesus' mission and ministry in the world. Just as the Holy Spirit descended on Jesus at the beginning of his public ministry and transformed the fearful disciples at Pentecost, the Spirit equips every Christian for a life of service and witness.

Many Catholics have come to realize that expectant faith is necessary to receive and experience the full power of the Holy Spirit that is available in confirmation. Indeed, God does not restrict the experience of the Holy Spirit's presence and power to the actual time of receiving this sacrament. Acts 10:47 testifies to this, and so does the experience of many confirmed Catholics who have been "baptized in the Holy Spirit" and have thus come to know the presence and power of the Holy Spirit in a new or fuller way.

Nonetheless, Catholics believe and have witnessed that God desires to send the fullness of his Holy Spirit through confirmation, and that the manifestation and gifts of the Holy Spirit will be evident when this sacrament is approached with expectant faith and prayer.

Anointing of the Sick

The scriptural roots of the sacrament of anointing the sick are very clear: Jesus healed the sick and commanded and empowered his disciples to do the same. "And they cast out many demons and anointed with oil many that were sick and healed them" (Mk 6:13). The elders in the early church continued this practice: "Is any among you sick? Let him call for the elders of the church, and let them pray over him, anointing him with oil in the name of the Lord, and the prayer of faith will save the sick man, and the Lord will raise him up; and if he has committed sins, he will be forgiven." (Jas 5:14-15)

This sacrament has been practiced since the earliest days of the church, but its focus has shifted at times. Until recently the emphasis was on preparation for death, but the Second Vatican Council restored an emphasis on prayer for physical and spiritual healing for all seriously ill persons. This sacrament does not preclude the importance of individual Christians praying for the sick, or even anointing them with blessed oil. It simply acknowledges Jesus' command to his apostles to anoint and heal the sick, and recognizes the power that has always been at work through their ministry and through that of the elders who succeeded them.

The sacrament does not guarantee that every sick person will be healed in a particular way. God's ways are above our ways, and often God will allow sickness or suffering to continue, and yet will work on a deeper level in the person. Many texts in the New Testament exhort Christians to rejoice in their sufferings, and to consider them a sharing in the suffering of Christ. (Rom 8:16, 17; Col 1:24; 2 Tm 2:11, 12; 1 Pt 4:13; 2 Cor 4:16-18). And yet, our God is a healing God, and he often responds to the prayer of Christians and works through the sacrament of the anointing of the sick to restore to health those who are suffering. Catholics will see the power of God manifest as they pray for the sick with expectant faith, and call upon his healing power through this sacrament.

The Sacrament of Holy Orders

From among his many followers, Jesus set apart certain men—especially "the Twelve"—to have a unique responsibility to carry on his mission and ministry. To prepare them for this Jesus gave them special formation, and authority to forgive sins, to preside over the breaking of the bread (the Eucharist) in his memory, and to instruct and guide new disciples.

The original apostles insured the continuation of the church's leadership by appointing elders to succeed them, and by conferring upon these elders the same authority that Jesus had given to them. By the late first century A.D., these elders were known as bishops, presbyters, and deacons. By the middle of the second century, a "three-tiered" leadership structure—a single bishop in each local church, assisted by presbyters and deacons—was the norm for the entire Christian world. The Catholic Church has preserved this basic pattern of official leadership and succession from the first or second century to the present day.

The apostles and the elders they appointed passed on their authority and ministry to others in a certain way. In the New Testament, the apostles were set apart for ministry by the prayer, fasting, and the "laying on of hands" of the Christian community. In the Acts of the Apostles, for example, the first deacons were "ordained" in this way: "and they chose Stephen, a man full of faith and of the Holy Spirit, and Philip, and Prochorus, and Nicanor, and Timon, and Parmenas, and Nicolaus, a proselyte of Antioch. These they set before the apostles, and they prayed and laid their hands upon them"

(Acts 6:5-6). In Acts 13, "while they were worshipping the Lord and fasting, the Holy Spirit said, 'set apart for me Barnabas and Saul for the work to which I have called them.' Then after fasting and praying they laid their hands on them and sent them off." (Acts 13:2, 3) St. Paul laid hands on Timothy to set him apart for the ministry, and reminded him ". . . to rekindle the gift of God that is within you through the laying on of my hands; for God did not give us a spirit of timidity but a spirit of power and love and self-control. . . . You then, my son, be strong in the grace that is in Christ Jesus, and what you have heard from me before many witnesses entrust to faithful men who will be able to teach others also." (2 Tm 1:6, 7; 2:1, 2)

Jesus set apart the apostles to lead the early church, instructed them, and after his resurrection breathed the Spirit upon them to empower them for this ministry. The apostles laid hands on the elders they selected to continue their ministry, and so the sacrament of "holy orders" or ordination was begun.

Jesus' priesthood is shared in some way by all believers, since the whole church is "a chosen race, a royal priesthood, a holy nation, God's own people" (1 Pt 2:9). And yet there have always been apostles and elders who have shared in Christ's priesthood in a unique way. The requirements for these offices in the primitive church are spelled out in the pastoral epistles, as described in Chapter Four.

One notable qualification for ordained ministry in the primitive church was that a bishop or deacon be "the husband of one wife." How then did the requirement of celibacy for priestly ministry arise in the Catholic Church? The Bible testifies to the fact that Jesus valued celibacy. Not only was Jesus himself celibate or "single for the Lord," but he taught,

Not everyone can accept this teaching, but only those to whom it has been given. For some are eunuchs because they were born that way; others were made that way by men; and others have renounced marriage because of the kingdom of heaven. The one who can accept this should accept it.

(Mt 19:11, 12)

Likewise, St. Paul instructed:

> I say this by way of concession, not of command. I wish that all were as I myself am. But each has his own special gift from God, one of one kind and one of another. . . .
>
> I want you to be free from anxieties. The unmarried man is anxious about the affairs of the Lord, how to please the Lord, but the married man is anxious about worldly affairs, how to please his wife, and his interests are divided. . . . I say this for your own benefit, not to lay any restraint upon you, but to promote good order and to secure your undivided devotion to the Lord . . . (1 Cor 7:6, 7, 32-34a, 35)

Jesus and Paul both make it clear that celibacy is not a call given to everyone, but that it is a gift that enables a person to devote his or her undivided attention to the affairs of the Lord and his kingdom. Since the early church men and women have committed themselves to God in this way, and so it should not be surprising that by the tenth century the Catholic Church of the Latin rite confirmed the single state of life as a requirement for the priesthood. The primary reason for this requirement is the imitation of Jesus. Celibacy is also a sign or a witness to the world. It involves renouncing some undeniably good things, sexual pleasure within marriage and the good of married life, for another good: greater freedom to devote time and attention to the Lord and to the building up of his body, the church.

However, it must be understood that celibacy is not an *absolute* requirement for priesthood. The Eastern rites of the Catholic Church allow married men to be ordained to the priesthood. This practice reflects their culture and Christian tradition, just as celibacy reflects the call of God to the Western "branch" of the Catholic Church, Roman Catholicism. Celibacy is a requirement that Roman Catholics teach and respect because of the biblical evidence for the value of celibacy, and its successful practice over many centuries.

The Catholic understanding of priesthood poses difficulties for many Christians. Besides the requirements of celibacy in the Roman Catholic Church, some Christians object that even to call a priest "father" violates Jesus' command in Matthew 23:9, "And call no man your father on earth, for you have one Father, who is in heaven." The Catholic understanding of Jesus' teaching is that no human being may be given the honor and respect due only to God the Father. However, even the apostle Paul told the Corinthians:

> For though you have countless guides in Christ, you do not have many fathers. For I became your father in Christ Jesus through the gospel. (1 Cor 4:14-15. See also 1 Thes 2:9-12)

It is in this Pauline sense that Catholics apply the title "father" to priests.

Other Christians are confused by the various titles of ordained ministers in the Catholic Church: priests, bishops, archbishops, abbots, cardinals, monks, and so on. These titles distinguish the different roles, orders, or offices of these ministers. The important thing is that they all share in the one priesthood of Jesus Christ as ministers set apart for leadership and service in the body of Christ. In the Catholic understanding, the bishops (a category which includes the pope, archbishops, and most cardinals) possess "the fullness of the sacrament of [holy] orders," while priests and deacons share in and extend the priestly ministry of their bishop.[12] This understanding is based on the way ordained leadership actually evolved and functioned in the early centuries of

Christianity, which Catholics believe was directed by the Holy Spirit of God.

Another Catholic Christian practice that is often questioned is the requirement that only men be ordained to the priesthood. The Catholic tradition here is based on the practice of Jesus. Jesus had many women disciples or followers, and his openness to women and his recognition of their human dignity stands in striking contrast to his culture, in which women were often treated like property or slaves. No one can accuse Jesus of refusing to "ordain" women because he was bound by the culture of his time in the way he related to them. The fact is that in spite of the evident respect that Jesus had for women, he did not select a woman to be among his twelve apostles. The early church followed his practice. Although many influential women are mentioned and described in the New Testament, there is no evidence that there were woman apostles, bishops, or priests. Woman deacons or "deaconesses" and other influential Christian women are mentioned in the New Testament (1 Tm 3:11; Rom 16:1), as well as in later Christian writings. But no women priests are mentioned, even in the later periods of the church's early development.

Because there is no precedent for the ordination of women to priesthood in either the Bible or during the first nineteen centuries of the church, the Catholic Church continued its practice of ordaining only men to this office. This does *not* mean that the Spirit of God could never lead the elders of the Catholic Church to change this practice, but it probably would have to be a very clear and convincing sign from the Lord that would impel the pope and Catholic bishops to overturn a practice so deeply rooted in the Catholic Christian tradition, and attested to by the scriptures themselves.

It is easy today to focus on these external qualifications for a Roman Catholic priest, celibate and male, and to neglect the more important spiritual qualities that a priest must possess and live out. A priest must be a man of prayer, a witness to Christ and his gospel, and a servant-leader of the Christian community. Through the sacrament of Holy Orders, the priest is set apart by God and by the Christian community to fulfill a special role in the body of Christ. The model for that role is Jesus himself, who laid down his life for his sheep. The priest is empowered by God, just as Jesus' first apostles were, to carry out the very mission that Jesus himself performed. They are to proclaim the Good News of the Kingdom, to teach with authority, to forgive sins, to pray with others for healing and deliverance from evil spirits, and to do the other work of Jesus' mission on earth. The priest, through his ordination, has also received the authority that Jesus gave to the twelve at the Last Supper to offer the bread and wine of the Eucharist to the Father in Jesus' name. He told them to "Do this in memory of me."

The priest should be expectant about the power of God available to him, for Jesus told his disciples that if they had faith in him they would do even greater works than he did (Jn 14:12). The core of the ministry of the priest may be summed up in the words of Acts 6, "prayer and ministry of the word." When a bishop ordains a man in the Sacrament of Holy Orders, he is set apart for priestly ministry, and is empowered to carry it out by the grace of God.

The Sacrament of Matrimony

Many Christians recognize marriage as an important part of Christian life, but Roman Catholics consider it a sacrament. They believe this because Jesus Christ has raised marriage to a new level. The roots of Christian marriage are found in the Old Testament, and confirmed by Jesus:

Have you not read that the creator from the beginning "made them male and female" and that he said: "This is why a man must leave father and mother, and cling to his wife, and the two become one body?" They are no longer two, therefore, but one body. So then, what God has united, man must not divide. (Mt 19:4-6)

Why is marriage a sacrament? First, because it is an action of God: "what *God* has united, man must not divide." Jesus is adamant about this, and re-established the indissolubility of marriage that existed before the fall of man:

> "It was because you were so unteachable," he said, "that Moses allowed you to divorce your wives, but it was not like this from the beginning. Now I say to you: The man who divorces his wife—I am not speaking of fornication—and marries another, is guilty of adultery." (Mt 19:8-9)

Marriage is a sacrament because Jesus invests it with a new grace and power which existed only "in the beginning," when God directly gave this grace of fidelity to Adam and Eve before their sin. Now it is only through God's power, conferred in this sacrament, that two human beings are able to faithfully live out this high calling to become "one flesh."

Marriage is also a sacrament because it is a visible, outward sign of Jesus' presence and love in the world. The love of a husband for his wife, for example, is a sign of Christ's love for the church:

> Husbands should love their wives just as Christ loved the Church and sacrificed himself for her, to make her holy.... A man never hates his own body, but he feeds it and looks after it, and that is the way Christ treats the Church, because it is his body—and we are its living parts... This mystery has many implications; but I am saying it applies to Christ and the Church. (Eph 5:25, 29, 30, 32)

Jesus confers a special grace which enables a Christian couple to be faithful for life, and consequently he expects and demands that we live according to the grace and power he provides. Divorce may have been tolerable before Jesus' coming, but now it is forbidden because of the grace of Jesus Christ, available through this sacrament. A husband is given the call and power to love his wife as Christ loved the church— even to the point of death. And wives, likewise, are called to love and submit to their husbands as the church loves and submits to Christ.

Were marriage not a sacrament with special graces given by God, all this would be impossible. But because marriage was established by Jesus to be a lasting sign of his love for the church, it has been raised by him to a new level—the level of a sacrament. Hence, what God has joined together, man must not divide.

The Sacraments Are Gifts

The sacraments are great gifts of God. Through them, the Lord offers us a share in his own life and power. Certainly the sacraments are not "magic." They have the full effect that God intends only when they are approached with expectant faith. Neither are the sacraments the *only* way that God works. Christians know that the Lord also freely shares his life and bestows his Holy Spirit in other ways, such as through prayer and faith-filled life in the Christian community. Nevertheless, the Bible makes it clear that God lowered himself to assume our human nature, and now chooses to communicate his life and love through ordinary, natural signs: water, oil, bread, wine, and simple human gestures and interaction. These signs, when properly enacted, become channels of God's abundant life through the merits of Jesus Christ. He is the greatest sacrament of God's saving love and the founder and life-source of all the sacraments.

EIGHT

The Communion of Saints

THE APOSTLE PAUL WROTE to the Gentiles who believed in Jesus: ". . . You are no longer strangers and sojourners, but you are fellow citizens with the saints and members of the household of God, built upon the foundations of the apostles and prophets, Christ Jesus himself being the cornerstone" (Eph 2:19-20).

Who are those "saints" that Paul mentions? Catholics usually use the word "saint" to refer to people of outstanding holiness, especially those they believe to be with the Lord in heaven.Sometimes we hear an exceptionally holy person on earth called a "saint," like Mother Teresa of Calcutta. In the New Testament, however, the word has a broader meaning. Paul called *all* his fellow believers "saints," not just the notably holy ones (see Rom 12:13, 16:15; 1 Cor 16:1, 15; 2 Cor 1:1; Eph 1:1; Phil 1:1; 4:21-22; Phlm 5). Some Bibles translate "saints" as "holy ones," which has the same meaning. This is also what the Apostles' Creed, one of the earliest statements of Christian faith means when it proclaims: "I believe in the communion of saints."

The phrase "the communion of saints" refers to the bond of unity among all those, living and dead, who are or have been committed followers of Jesus Christ. St. Paul's favorite image for this unity or communion is the "body of Christ." He says of believers that, "we, though many, are one body in Christ, and individually members of one another" (Rom 12:5). The members of Christ's body are so united that "if one member suffers, all suffer together" (1 Cor 12:26). Jesus prayed that his followers would be united to each other just as closely as he was united to the Father (see Jn 17:20-23).

This close, living unity among all who belong to God through Jesus is what the Creed calls "communion." When Catholics profess that they believe in the communion of saints, they are professing their unity with all the faithful followers of Jesus Christ.

Catholics also believe that the committed followers of Jesus who have died remain in communion with his followers still living on earth. From God's perspective, the distinction between his people who are "living" or "dead" in terms of their human, physical existence is not all that important. God is beyond time, and sees our human life on earth as a brief, fleeting phase in comparison with our total, eternal life as spiritual beings. We get a glimpse of this perspective from the teaching of Jesus, who insisted that those of God's people who have passed from this life are not dead. He told the Jews who did not believe this: "Have you not read in the book of Moses ... how God said to him, 'I am the God of Abraham, the God of Isaac, and the God of Jacob.' He is not the God of the dead, but of the living." (Mk 12:26-27; see also Lk 20:34-38; Mk 5:39; Mt 9:24; Lk 8:52). Those who are judged worthy of the resurrected life are alive to God (Lk 20:34-38). In fact, Jesus even demonstrated to Peter, James, and John that the "saints" of the Old Covenant are alive when he spoke with Moses and Elijah on the mountain of transfiguration (Mk 9:4). Jesus indicated that the "veil" that separates the "saints" on earth from those who have died physically is actually a rather thin one!

Therefore, Catholics believe that some of the "saints" who have passed from this life are now united to God in heaven.

The story of the "good thief" in Lk 23:43 illustrates this, for Jesus promised him "today you will be with me in paradise." Catholics also believe, as will be explained in the final chapter of this book, that some of the saints who have died undergo a final purification by God after their death, which prepares them to enter into the full glory of his presence in heaven.

For Catholics, the communion of saints includes *all* of God's people—those in heaven, those on earth, and even those in a state of purification (purgatory). All of these people are in a communion because they are all in a real relationship with God through Jesus Christ, and hence are "one body in Christ, and individually members of one another" (Rom 12:5). As the Second Vatican Council describes it, "At the present time some of (Jesus') disciples are pilgrims on earth. Others have died and are being purified, while still others are in glory beholding 'clearly God himself, three and one, as He is.' "[1]

Traditional Catholic theology has called those saints still on earth the "church militant" (still "fighting the good fight of faith"), those in purgatory the "church suffering," and those in heaven the "church triumphant." But these are not three distinct "churches," but together make up the one church of Jesus Christ: "All partake in the same love for God and neighbor, and all sing the same hymn of glory to our God."[2]

The Help of the Saints

Catholics believe that the communion of saints is much more than an interesting theological concept. Our communion with all of God's saints means that Christians alive today are not alone in the struggle against the world, the flesh, and Satan. Christians are part of a mighty army, spanning space and time, led by Jesus as our commander. We are part of a vast throng of angels and of saints who have lived before us.

C.S. Lewis vividly described how God might see all of his people as one vast, united family, bound together in a communion that transcends time. In his book, *The Screwtape*

Letters, Lewis has the demon Screwtape explain to a junior demon how Satan is aided by the narrow view of the church held by many Christians:

> One of our great allies at present is the church itself. Do not misunderstand me. I do not mean the church as we see her spread out through all time and space and rooted in eternity, terrible as an army with banners. That, I confess, is a spectacle that makes our boldest tempters uneasy. But fortunately it is quite invisible to these humans.[3]

Fortunately for the demons, perhaps, but unfortunately for the Christians! One of Satan's chief strategies to defeat the church is to divide and isolate its members from one another and thus deprive them of the strength they can receive from their fellow members of the communion of saints.

The next question that naturally arises is, how can Christians draw upon this support?

An important way is to reflect on the example of the lives of the saints, both in heaven and on earth. Chapter eleven of the Letter to the Hebrews calls to mind the faith and lives of the Old Testament "saints," and concludes with these stirring words: "Therefore, since we are surrounded by so great a cloud of witnesses, let us also lay aside every weight, and sin which clings so closely, and let us run with perseverance the race that is set before us. . ." (Heb 12:1). The saints are witnesses that the life of faith and Christian perfection is possible. God expects his followers to lead lives of exemplary holiness. Jesus himself taught, "you, therefore, must be perfect, as your heavenly Father is perfect" (Mt 5:48), and Paul agreed that we must "make holiness perfect in the fear of God" (2 Cor 7:1).

Those whom the Catholic Church officially recognizes as "saints" are those men and women whose lives have been outstanding and heroic examples of Christian perfection and holiness. The process of "canonization" is the way that the Catholic Church discerns which people have lived such outstandingly holy lives on earth that they must certainly be with the Lord in glory, now that they have died. This custom of honoring particularly holy people with the title of "saint" reaches back to the first centuries of Christianity. It initially arose as the church remembered and honored the lives of the apostles and the martyrs who sacrificed their lives rather than abandon their faith in Jesus (see Rv 6:9-11, 7:13-15).[4]

The process of canonization involves a careful investigation of the life of a person who has died to determine whether God has attested to their holiness through miracles, conversions, examples of exceptional holiness, and many other indicators. Those who are canonized, or officially recognized as saints by the Catholic Church, represent only a few outstanding examples of the myriad of other holy men and women who are fully united with the Lord. The canonized saints are not meant to be looked upon as an exclusive "club," but as examples and models of holiness, representing all of the saints in heaven. The diversity of the canonized saints provides models for every Christian. Some saints led public lives and consulted with thousands of people while they lived. Other saints were obscure or little-known during their lives, but later their holiness was acknowledged by reports about their lives or by miracles worked through their prayers of intercession to God. The canonized saints include people from every state or situation of life: men and women, married and celibate, "active" and "contemplative" Christians, young and old, rich and poor, beggars and kings.

But why should Christians "imitate" the saints at all? Shouldn't we model ourselves after Jesus? Isn't he our only model?

Of course Jesus Christ is the ultimate model for all Christians, but he is not our only model. His life is reflected in splendid and varied ways in the lives of those of the past and present who earnestly follow him. This is another illustration of the incarnational principle. God works through his body, the church, and through the human beings who make up the church. He knows that as human beings we necessarily model our lives on the lives of other persons, both living and dead. Indeed, one of the reasons why we imitate Jesus Christ is to reflect his life to those around us. As St. Paul boldly said, "Be imitators of me as I am of Christ" (1 Cor 11:1), and "Brethren, join in imitating me and mark those who so live as you have an example in us" (Phil 3:17). The Second Vatican Council expressed this point well:

> For when we look at the lives of those who have faithfully followed Christ, we are inspired with a new reason for seeking the city which is to come (Heb 13:14, 11:10). At the same time we are shown a most safe path by which ... we will be able to arrive at perfect union with Christ, that is holiness. In the lives of those who shared in our humanity and yet were transformed into especially successful images of Christ (cf. 2 Cor 3:18), God vividly manifests to men his presence and his face. He speaks to us in them, and gives us a sign of his kingdom, to which we are powerfully drawn, surrounded as we are by so many witnesses (cf. Heb. 12:1), and having such an argument for the truth of the gospel.[5]

The Intercession of the Saints

Another way that the members of the communion of saints can support one another is by praying for each other. Most of us have asked another Christian—another "saint" in the body of Christ—to pray for us when we have had a particular need. The apostle Paul frequently asked other disciples of Jesus to pray for him (see Col 4:3; Rom 15:30-32; 1 Thes 5:25; 2 Thes 1:11, 3:1; Eph 6:19). Other New Testament writers also urge us to pray for each other for healing or deliverance from sin (Jas 5:13-18; 1 Jn 5:16). Prayer seems to be a normal way for the saints on earth to support each other.

Catholics believe that if we ask our fellow saints on earth to pray for us, we should also be able to ask for prayers from the saints who are already united with the Lord. If the prayers of certain Christians here on earth seem to have special power because of their great faith or holiness, how much more powerful and effective are the prayers of those who are fully united to God in heaven!

The Bible says little about the intercession of the saints in heaven. Jesus spoke of Abraham, Isaac and Jacob (the "saints" of the Old Covenant) as being alive to God (Mk 12:26-27) and he himself conversed with Elijah and Moses on the mountain (Mt 17:3). However, the Book of Revelation frequently mentions the twenty-four elders (representing all the saints in heaven) gathered around God's throne engaged in exuberant praise. In one passage, Rev. 5:8, John mentions that these elders possessed "golden bowls full of incense, which are the prayers of the saints." The New Testament usage of "saint" usually refers to Jesus' disciples on earth, so here we have a beautiful image of intercession: the twenty-four elders (the "saints" in heaven) offering the prayers of the "saints" on earth before the throne of God like sweet-smelling incense. It is also clear from early Christian tradition that the Church believed in the intercession of the saints in heaven. For example, when a certain teacher questioned the practice of asking the saints in heaven to pray for them, St. Jerome replied:

> You say in your book that while we live we are able to pray for each other, but afterwards when we have died, the prayer of no person for another can be heard.... But if the apostles and martyrs while still in the body can pray for others, at a time when they ought still to be solicitous about themselves, how much more will they do so after their crowns, victories, and triumphs?[6]

The practice of honoring the saints in heaven and asking for their prayers can be abused. Some Christians think that such practices amount to idolatry—worshipping men instead of God. In the fifth century, St. Augustine warned against any devotion to the saints becoming a form of worship:

We, the Christian community, assemble to celebrate the memory of the martyrs with ritual solemnity because we want to be inspired to follow their example, share in their merits, and be helped by their prayers. Yet we erect no altars to any of the martyrs—although (they are erected) in their memory—but to God himself, the God of those martyrs.

No bishop, when celebrating at an altar where these holy bodies rest has ever said, "Peter, we make this offering to you," or "Paul, to you," or "Cyprian, to you." No, what is offered is offered always to God, who crowned the martyrs. . . .

So we venerate the martyrs with the same veneration of love and fellowship that we give to the holy men of God still with us. . . . But the veneration strictly called "worship," or *latria*, that is, the special homage belonging only to the divinity, is something we give and teach others to give to God alone. The offering of a sacrifice belongs to worship in this sense (that is why those who sacrifice to idols are called idol-worshippers), and we neither make nor tell others to make any such offering to any martyr, any holy soul, or any angel. . .

The saints themselves forbid anyone to offer them the worship they know is reserved for God, as is clear from the case of Paul and Barnabas (see Acts 14:8-18).[7]

Following the teaching given here by St. Augustine and many other teachers, Catholics venerate and honor those saints but do not worship them. The saints in heaven can pray or intercede to God for us, and we can ask them to pray for us, just as we can ask a fellow Christian to pray for us. The intercession of the saints and of Mary on our behalf does not detract from the unique mediation of Jesus, any more than asking someone here on earth to pray for us would.

However, worship is due only to God. All Christian prayer, whether the prayer of the saints in heaven or of Mary, the mother of the Lord, or of us saints here on earth, is directed to the Father through Jesus Christ, who is the "one mediator between God and men" (1 Tm 2:5).

Images, Relics, and Prayers for the Dead

Catholics sometimes make use of statues, images, medals, relics, and other objects to call to mind their relationship with the saints of the past. These objects are intended to recall the example of the particular saint, and to remind us of their nearness to God and their power to intercede for us on earth. Again, this is the incarnational principle at work. God works through human beings and earthly things. Statues, images, relics, and the like remind us of our living relationship with God and with the saints who have gone before us.

Catholics use certain objects to recall departed members of the communion of saints in a way similar to a family's use of pictures or other remembrances of loved ones. The "communion of saints" means that the followers of Jesus are all part of one great family, of which God is Father. Statues and medals remind us of the other great members of God's family whom we admire and desire to imitate, and whom we approach to pray for us. In the same way, the members of a large and close-knit human family keep pictures of other family mem-·bers, gifts they have given, and other visible signs of membership in the family. Catholics do not worship pictures and statues of great saints and holy people any more than they worship pictures of departed family members on the walls and tables in their homes. There have been exaggerations and abuses of these things among Catholics, but, when used properly, these images lead Catholics to praise God more (not less) because they reflect the richness and diversity of God's work through his people.

Finally, a word should be added about "relics." Relics are remains of saints such as bones, ashes, clothing or even writings or belongings left behind. The early Christians showed honor to the departed saints by respecting these remains. Again, this is a very human response. We bury the dead with respect and treasure the things left behind by a departed loved one because we love and honor them. However, there was also a spiritual reason for the early Christians' treatment of the relics of the saints. Miracles were frequently reported by those who came in contact with these remains. This should not be surprising. After all, people had been healed by touching Jesus' outer garments (Mk 5:25-34), and the Acts of the Apostles reported that healings and exorcisms occurred when people touched handkerchiefs or aprons to Paul's body and brought them to the sick (Acts 19:11-12).

Through the centuries, similar miracles have been worked when relics of deceased saints have been brought to the sick, possessed, or dying. God continues to work in a "sacramental" way—using things as well as people to communicate his power. Of course, there is a danger of lapsing into superstition here. Catholics must avoid it, remembering that it is God's power alone that brings about all healings and miracles. Relics themselves contain no "magic" power, but God uses them to testify to the spiritual power released through the life of an exceptionally holy man or woman.

Besides asking the prayers of the saints in heaven, Christians from the earliest centuries of the church have also expressed their communion with those who have died by praying for the dead. Inscriptions in the Roman catacombs indicate that the early Christians honored and prayed for their deceased relatives and friends. Around 211 A.D., Tertullian wrote that Christians offered prayer and the Eucharist for the deceased on the anniversaries of their death.[8] St. Augustine wrote, "Neither are the souls of the pious dead separated from the church, which even now is the kingdom of Christ. Otherwise there would be no remembrance of them at the altar of God in the communication of the Body of Christ."[9]

In praying for the dead the early Christians were expressing their belief that departed brothers and sisters underwent a purification after death that we call purgatory. Their prayers were prayers that God would have mercy on them during this time of healing and purification.

The Second Vatican Council reaffirmed the belief of the early church that Christians ought to pray for those who are experiencing God's purification after death: "Very much aware of the bonds linking the whole mystical body of Jesus Christ, the pilgrim church from the very first ages of the Christian religion has cultivated with great piety the memory of the dead. Because it is 'a holy and wholesome thought to pray for the dead that they may be loosed from sins' (2 Mc 12:46), she has also offered prayers for them."[10]

God's Family

To understand the communion of saints, we should think of it as God's family. Some members of the family are living here on earth; these Christians naturally tend to relate to each other and seek one another's help in striving to do God's will. Other family members have completed this life on earth and are fully united with the Father in heaven. Through the Holy Spirit, who binds the whole family together, Christians can relate with these "glorified" brothers and sisters and seek their guidance and prayers, just as we can do with those "family members" on earth. (We should begin now to get acquainted with them, since we will soon spend eternity with them!) The third branch of the family are those who have died but are not yet fully purified from the sin of this life. They are awaiting entry into the full glory of God's kingdom. This branch of the family of God will be discussed more fully in the final chapter of this book. Christians have long believed that they could aid these Christians in purgatory by praying for them.

Honor paid to the saints does not detract from honor due God. Indeed, God is glorified in the proper honor given to his people, because he has chosen to identify himself with them through his Son, Jesus Christ. God is a Father who is glad when his children, either on earth or in heaven, praise each other's virtues, seek each other's help, and support each other through their prayers to him. In the mutual love of those in heaven, in purgatory, and on earth, the body of Christ is strengthened and grows up "into him who is the head, into Christ" (Eph 4:15).

Christians can also look forward in hope to that great day when all the saints will be gathered around God's throne to praise him forever. Then we will join our voices with "the mighty voice of a great multitude in heaven crying: 'Hallelujah! Salvation and glory and power belong to our God'" (Rv 19:1).

That day will be the most glorious "family reunion" of all—far exceeding our greatest hope and imagination.

NINE

Mary

I T IS A TRAGIC FACT that beliefs about Mary, the mother of Jesus, have become a source of division among Christians. Many Christians honestly do not understand what Catholics believe about Mary and why. Sometimes Catholics have been accused of worshipping Mary. For their part, many Catholics do not understand why other Christians are sensitive to the attention given to Mary by Catholics. Indeed, many Catholics do not understand what their own church teaches about Mary, and are thus ill-equipped to explain these beliefs to others. This chapter is intended to help bridge this chasm of misunderstanding.

Mary and the "Hierarchy of Truths"

As explained in the prologue, Catholics believe that there is a "hierarchy" or order of Christian truths. In other words, not all Christian truths are equally central to the basic Gospel message. Official Catholic teaching has never considered beliefs about Mary as being equal in importance to truths about God—the Father, Son, and Holy Spirit. Truths about Mary are all related to the basic gospel message, though they are not the primary focus of the gospels. This principle has its foundation in the Bible. For example, in all the New Testament letters attributed to Paul, Mary is mentioned only once, and not even by name (Gal 4:4). This certainly does not prove that

Paul never spoke about Mary, but it does indicate that the basic gospel could be proclaimed without focusing on Mary.

However, many other New Testament writings *do* speak about Mary, and Catholic Christians therefore believe that it is important to have a correct understanding of her role in God's plan of salvation. The Catholic Church has never ceased to teach about Mary, and in the past 150 years it has made some major pronouncements about her life and her role in God's saving plan. Catholics believe that the church's understanding about Mary, as about all Christian truth, has deepened and become more precise over time through the guidance of the Holy Spirit. Beliefs about her have been clarified to answer new questions and to settle new controversies. When the Catholic Church appears to teach "new things" about Mary, it is usually an official statement or clarification of things that have long been taught and believed by Christians. These statements usually present truths that originated in the church during the early centuries of Christianity.

The principle of the "hierarchy" of truths points out two extremes that must be avoided in Christian teaching about Mary. On the one hand, Marian doctrines must not be presented as equal in importance to the fundamental Christian truths about the nature of God and redemption. Mary must never be exalted to the status of a "goddess" deserving the worship and adoration due only to God. On the other hand, Mary's role in God's plan of salvation must not be ignored nor neglected.

The role of Mary may not be among the "ten most central Christian truths," but neither is it a Christian truth of little importance or consequence for Christians and their daily lives. The Catholic Church believes, as we shall see, that God intends Mary to have a definite place and role in the life of every Christian.

The Second Vatican Council urged the theologians and preachers of the Catholic Church to avoid these extremes:

This Synod earnestly exhorts theologians and preachers of

the divine word that in treating of the unique dignity of the Mother of God, they carefully and equally avoid the falsity of exaggeration on the one hand, and the excess of narrow-mindedness on the other. . . . Pursuing the study of the sacred scripture, the holy Fathers, the doctors and liturgies of the church, and under the guidance of the church's teaching authority, let them rightly explain the offices [roles] and privileges of the Blessed Virgin which are always related to Christ, the source of all truth, sanctity, and piety.[1]

The Council briefly mentions here the key principle for understanding doctrines about Mary: they must always be related to Jesus Christ, who is "the source of all truth, sanctity, and piety."

Fr. Kilian McDonnell, O.S.B., summarizes the approach of Catholic Christians to Mary in relationship to the hierarchy of truths:

> Most Catholic theologians would grant that the role of Mary represents a secondary truth in a hierarchy of New Testament truths. At the top of that ladder of truths comes the Fatherhood of God, the death and resurrection of Jesus, the power and gifts of the Spirit, the forgiveness of sins, and the promises of eternal life. Mary's role does not have the same "weight" in the New Testament witness as these truths and events.
>
> Yet her role should not be considered Roman Catholic denominational baggage, a Catholic belief but not a Christian belief. The easy distinction between a Catholic truth and a Christian truth is not acceptable. The role of Mary, it is our contention, is specifically a Christian truth. Obviously, one does not want to say that Protestants who do not accept Mary's role are not Christian, rather, the assertion is that her role belongs to the total Christian mystery, and therefore to the definition of a Christian. . . .
>
> Over the centuries the experience of millions of Christians witnesses to the role of Mary. That experience is

manifested, in part, in the liturgies of the Eastern and Western church. Will not contemporary Christian life be impoverished if that whole experience is dismissed without the most careful discernment?[2]

While Christians must not exaggerate the importance of the role of Mary in God's plan, neither can they afford to dismiss it. Let us begin this "careful discernment" of Mary's role that Fr. McDonnell calls for by examining the New Testament.

Mary's Role in God's Plan of Salvation

A careful study of the New Testament reveals a development or unfolding of the Holy Spirit's revelation to the church about the identity and importance of Mary. If one were only to judge by the earlier writings of the New Testament, a person might conclude that Mary wasn't too important. Paul, as we have said, hardly mentions Mary, and the Gospel of Mark, probably the earliest Gospel written, presents Mary in a seemingly negative light, as one of Jesus' relatives who did not understand him or his mission. This is not surprising; according to Mark's Gospel, *no one* really understood Jesus or his mission, not even his closest apostles, until his crucifixion.

However, the later writings of the New Testament, especially the Gospels of Luke and John, present Mary as having a positive and even prominent role in God's plan of salvation. Apparently, the Holy Spirit guided the authors of these gospels into an understanding of Mary and her role that is fuller than the earlier New Testament writings. Catholics view this development as a work of the Holy Spirit. Later doctrinal definitions concerning Mary by church councils and popes are a continuation of the Holy Spirit's work, leading the church into the fullness of truth about Mary and her role in God's plan of salvation.

All Catholic Christian beliefs about Mary are basically rooted in God's revelation in the Bible. The Bible presents Mary as a person whom God set apart to play a vital role in his plan of salvation. God honored Mary by eternally predestining her to be the mother of the Savior—the one through whom God himself would enter into human history. What greater gift or dignity could God give to a human being? This honor given to Mary reveals the dignity of all women; a woman is more important in God's saving plan than any angel or other spiritual being.

Mary's role in God's plan was prophetically foreshadowed in the Old Testament. In the book of Genesis, God tells the serpent (Satan): "I will put enmity between you and the woman, and between your offspring and hers; he will crush your head, and you will strike his heel" (Gn 3:15). The offspring of the woman (Mary) is Jesus, who came to crush the head of the serpent, to defeat Satan and his work. The prophet Isaiah spoke of a sign that the Lord would give to Israel: "the virgin shall be with child, and bear a son, and shall name him Immanuel" ("God with us") (Is 7:14). The gospel of Matthew presents Jesus' birth of Mary as a fulfillment of this prophecy (Mt 1:22-23). Some Christians have also interpreted the "daughter of Zion" theme in the Old Testament as prefiguring Mary's role. The angel Gabriel greeted Mary, "Rejoice, O highly favored daughter! The Lord is with you." (Lk 1:28)

Mary's Response to God

God had chosen Mary from before all time to be the mother of the Savior, but her response to God's call was crucial. She freely chose to accept God's plan for her life. The angel Gabriel appeared to this young girl and announced that she was to bear a son (Lk 1:26-33). Mary, being a virgin, was naturally perplexed and responded, "How can this be since I do not know man?" (Lk 1:34). After Gabriel explained that "the Holy Spirit will come upon you and the power of the Most High will overshadow you" (Lk 1:35ff), Mary's reponse was simple and full of faith: "I am the servant of the Lord. Let it be done to me as you say" (Lk 1:38).

Catholics honor Mary because of this great faith and obedience. Many early Christian writers noted that God allowed his whole plan of salvation to hinge on Mary's free response to Gabriel's message. Because of her "yes" to God, Mary is the new Eve, reversing the first Eve's "no."[3] By the disobedience of Eve, all mankind became immersed in the bondage of sin. Mary's obedience to God opened the way for the saving work of Jesus. As St. Irenaeus explained late in the second century, "The knot of Eve's disobedience was loosed by the obedience of Mary. What the virgin Eve had bound in unbelief, the virgin Mary loosed through faith."[4]

Mary responded to God in her great prayer of praise, the "Magnificat" (Lk 1:46-55). She acknowledged the honor God had given her—"all ages to come shall call me blessed" (1:48). But she immediately directed all praise for this back to God— "for he who is mighty has done great things for me, and holy is his name" (1:49).

Mary's "yes" to God brought her hardship and suffering as well as honor. She gave birth to Jesus in a stable, then had to flee to Egypt to escape Herod's wrath (see Mt 2:13-14; Lk 2:6-7). When Mary and Joseph presented Jesus in the temple, Simeon prophesied that she would be "pierced with a sword" (Lk 2:35). She witnessed her son's death. Mary also experienced the normal anxieties of a mother, as when the 12-year-old Jesus was lost in Jerusalem (see Lk 2:41-50). Yet scripture never shows her complaining about these trials. Rather, Mary "kept all these things, pondering them in her heart" (Lk 2:19, 51).

Mary and Her Son

The Bible states clearly that Mary is not blessed simply because she had a "blood" or biological relationship to Jesus. In Luke's gospel, a woman cried out to Jesus, "Blest is the womb that bore you and the breasts that nursed you." Jesus replied, "Rather blessed are they who hear the word of God and keep it" (Lk 11:22-28). Luke was not implying that Mary,

Jesus' mother, was not blessed; in fact, he states elsewhere that Mary is highly favored by God (1:28-30). The point is that even though it was a privilege to bear Jesus in her womb, Mary is even more to be honored because her life was devoted to doing the will of God: "I am the servant of the Lord" (Lk 1:38).

The later gospels (Luke and John) present Mary as a model disciple of her Son. Although she does not appear often in the accounts of Jesus' public ministry, it is evident that she was profoundly united to his person and work. She followed her son from the beginning to the end of his life. We find her at Cana (see Jn 2:1-12), where her simple, firm faith evoked Jesus' first miracle. This scene gives us a glimpse of Mary's role of intercession—that she is able to approach Jesus with the needs of others, and she is heard for her faith.

At the end of Jesus' life, Mary was at the foot of the cross, a witness to his death. Artists have enshrined the moving scene of Jesus' lifeless body cradled in her arms, the "sword" Simeon prophesied "piercing her heart." Certainly Mary was a true disciple of her son, having a relationship with him that went beyond the purely human ties of mother and child.

Mary continued to be a disciple of her son after his death. She was with the apostles in the upper room in Jerusalem after Jesus' ascension, as they "devoted themselves to constant prayer" (Acts 1:14). Mary was evidently still among this group when they received the great outpouring of the Holy Spirit at Pentecost a few days later.

The Holy Spirit was no stranger to Mary. In fact, the New Testament records that she first received the Holy Spirit when she conceived Jesus, thus making her the first recipient of the Holy Spirit in the New Testament. Gabriel announced that "the Holy Spirit will come upon you, and the power of the Most High will overshadow you; hence the holy offspring to be born will be called Son of God" (Lk 1:35). The language of this announcement is very similar to the image of "power of the Most High" overshadowing the Ark of the Covenant in Exodus 40:34-35, or the Temple in 1 Kings 8:10. Through the power of the Spirit, Mary became the new Ark of the Covenant and the new Temple because God dwelt fully within her in Jesus.[5]

The result of the Spirit's dwelling in Mary was praise of God and prophecy. Mary's prophetic prayer of praise, the Magnificat (Lk 1:46-55), both glorifies God and prophesies the mission of Jesus to bring the good news to the poor and lowly. She also prophesied that, "all generations will call me blessed" (Lk 1:48), a prophecy which is fulfilled through all Christians who call Mary the "Blessed Virgin." Mary, then, is portrayed by the Bible as a woman filled with the Holy Spirit. This gift resulted in her bearing Jesus, the Son of God, and in her unique gifts of praise and prophecy. Many authors have noted that in the New Testament the presence of Mary often evokes (calls forth) the presence of the Holy Spirit.

Our Mother

Mary may be the mother of Jesus, but in what sense is she "our mother," the mother of Christians? The Catholic understanding of this term of honor is based on a passage of John's Gospel describing Jesus' words on the cross: "When Jesus saw his mother and the disciple whom he loved standing near, he said to his mother, 'Woman, behold your son!' Then he said to the disciple, 'Behold, your Mother.'" (Jn 19:26-27)

Catholics have long believed that this scene, coming at the very climax of John's narrative, holds a rich symbolic meaning. Jesus' last act upon the cross was to give Mary as a mother to all Jesus' faithful followers, symbolized by the "disciple whom he loved." And he gave Mary to all of us, the faithful disciples of Jesus symbolized by the "beloved disciple," to be her sons and daughters. For many centuries, Christians have looked to Mary as a mother and have experienced her help and care.

Obviously, Mary is not a "physical" mother to all Christians, but she is recognized as a mother "in faith" or "in the order of grace." This is so because of Jesus' words, and because of her special relationship with him. Christians have become the body of Christ and brothers and sisters to Jesus through his grace. In the same way and by the same grace, Mary has become the spiritual mother of every Christian, since she is the mother of Jesus Christ.[6]

A Correct Understanding of Mary's Role

Catholics honor Mary and look to her as our mother in faith but they do not worship Mary or "pray to Mary" as they pray to God. Worship belongs only to God. Catholics do ask Mary to pray for us, and believe that her intercession has a great effect in calling forth God's grace and mercy. But this is because of her her special relationship with Jesus, not because of her own merits.

The Second Vatican Council emphasized that Jesus remains the one mediator between God and man (1 Tm 2:5). Mary's intercession

in no way obscures or diminishes the unique mediation of Christ, but rather shows its power. For all the saving influences of the Blessed Virgin on men originate, not from some inner necessity, but from the divine pleasure. They flow forth from the superabundance of the merits of Christ, rest on his mediation, depend entirely on it, and draw all their power from it. In no way do they impede the immediate union of the faithful with Christ. Rather, they foster this union.[7]

God himself accomplishes and provides everything that mankind needs, but in the richness of his plan he also chooses to entrust his creatures with a share in his work. Jesus is the one great high priest (see Heb 8:1), and yet he calls Christians a "priestly people" and invites them to share in his priesthood (1 Pt 2:9). In the same way, Jesus, the "one mediator" entrusts a share in his work of mediation to his creatures by allowing and enabling us to pray to God for each other.

Catholics believe that Mary also has a special role of

intercession because of her special role in God's plan of salvation. Jesus and Mary are not in competition. Jesus is the source of all God's grace and salvation, and Mary directs her prayers and our attention to Jesus. The passage that calls Jesus the "one mediator" (1 Tm 2:1-6), also urges *all* Christians to bring "requests, prayers, intercession and thanksgiving" to God (1 Tm 2:1). Most of us have experienced how we can be channels of God's grace to others and how others can bring grace to us. Catholics believe that God has chosen to use Mary as a unique channel of the grace of her son because of her special relationship with him. He has given her a motherly concern for all his sons and daughters. Because of the eternal character of God's work, Mary was and is the mother of Jesus, and the mother of all believers. She is now with the Lord, continuing to intercede for the needs of God's people. As the Second Vatican Council stated:

> By her maternal love, Mary cares for the brethren of her son who still journey on earth.... Therefore, the Blessed Virgin is invoked by the church under the titles of Advocate, Auxiliatrix, Adjutrix, and Mediatrix. These, however, are to be so understood that they neither take away nor add anything to the dignity and efficacy of Christ, the one mediator. For no creature could ever be classed with the incarnate Word and Redeemer.[8]

When Mary is given such titles as "Mediatrix" or "Co-redemptress," extreme care must be taken to explain that Mary has only been given a share in the mediation and redemptive work of Jesus Christ. Nothing she has done or could do in herself merits or gives salvation. Like us, Mary only cooperates with God's grace and his saving plan. Her special role as an intercessor, a model disciple, and a mother to believers, only stems from God's sovereign choice and from his grace.

Catholics pay attention to Mary because she is a model of discipleship; she teaches us what it means and what it costs to follow Jesus. Mary is a model of the church, in that she shows concretely how we as human beings are to relate to God through Jesus. Mary is also a mother who leads us to understand and appreciate her Son. For all these reasons, Catholic Christians honor Mary. But ultimately she is honored simply because God has honored her by choosing her to be the mother of Jesus, Son of God.

Special Beliefs about Mary

Many Christians who honor Mary as a woman of faith and as a model disciple have difficulty understanding why the Catholic Church teaches certain other beliefs about Mary— that she was conceived without sin, for example, or that she was assumed into heaven at the end of her life on earth.

Where did these teachings come from? They are not explicitly taught in scripture, and it is not even historically clear that they were handed down from the preaching of the original apostles. Rather, these beliefs emerged over time as Christians reflected on what the Bible says about Jesus and his mother.

As the Christian people came to a deeper understanding of Jesus as the incarnate Son of God, they began to consider what this belief implied about Mary. For example, if Jesus was truly God, wasn't it correct to speak of his mother as the mother of God? Various phrases in the Bible, like the angel's greeting, "Hail, full of grace," took on the greater significance in light of these reflections.

As the teaching authorities of the Catholic Church discerned which beliefs about Mary were to be considered the authentic beliefs of the church, two principles of discernment guided their judgment. First, no Christian belief can contradict anything in the Bible or in the genuine tradition handed down from the apostles. All further understandings of Mary's role had to be tested against the canon of revealed truth. Secondly, any insight that develops from reflection on the Christian revelation must be shown to have won acceptance from God's people over a long period of time. Individual theologians can be wrong, no matter how convincing their arguments may seem. But God has promised to protect his church as a whole from error (see John 16:13). The fact that a teaching has been consistently accepted by the great pastors and teachers of Christian history, and by the people of the church as well, is a sign that the Holy Spirit was leading God's people to this insight.

Four particular teachings about Mary have met these criteria and are now part of the official teaching of the Catholic Church.

Mary As Ever-Virgin. Most Christians believe that Mary was a virgin before and at the time of the birth of her son Jesus (see Mt 1:18-25; Lk 1:26-27). Yet Catholics also believe that Mary remained a virgin for the rest of her life.

Why do Catholics believe this? What about the scripture texts that mention the brothers and sisters of Jesus (Mt 12:46; Mk 3:31, 6:3; Lk 8:19)? What about the statement that Joseph did not know (have sexual relations with) Mary "until she had borne a son" (Mt 1:25)? These statements seem to indicate that after Jesus' birth Mary and Joseph had a normal marriage and raised other children.

However, the belief that Mary was ever-virgin is very ancient. The great teachers of the church from at least the fourth century on spoke of Mary as having remained a virgin throughout her life. Those who proclaimed Mary's perpetual virginity include some of the most illustrious Christians of all time: Athanasius, Epiphanius, Jerome, Augustine, Cyril of Alexandria, and others. One of the early church councils, the Second Council of Constantiople (553-554 A.D.) twice referred to Mary as "ever-virgin." Even the Protestant reformers Martin Luther, John Calvin, and Huldreich Zwingli affirmed their belief in Mary's perpetual virginity.[9]

Were all these great Christians unaware of what the Bible teaches on this subject? Certainly not. The scripture passages that raise questions about Mary's perpetual virginity are not decisive. The Greek words for "brothers and sisters" (e.g., of

Jesus) were also used to refer to other close relatives—cousins, nephews and nieces, and so on. Regarding Matthew 1:25, the Greek and Semitic usage of the word "until" does not imply anything about what happens after the time indicated. In this case, there is no necessary implication that Joseph and Mary had sexual contact or other children after Jesus. In Matthew's Gospel it simply emphasizes that Mary was indeed a virgin at the time Jesus was born. Likewise, references to Jesus as a "first-born" do not imply that there was a second- or third-born.[10]

Indeed, leading Catholic and Protestant scholars agree that the New Testament does not give conclusive evidence either for or against the doctrine of Mary's perpetual virginity. In such cases Catholics have always sought to understand the scripture according to what the Holy Spirit has led the church as a whole to believe. Here it seems clear that the Christian people have historically believed that Mary remained a virgin.[11]

This belief is important because it emphasizes the uniqueness of Mary's call and mission: No other human was carried in the womb that bore God himself made man. Her virginity does not demean sex or marriage but proclaims the uniqueness of her call and the holiness of the God who dwelt within her. Catholics believe that Mary freely chose this virginity in order to honor God, just as she freely accepted God's invitation to be the mother of the Redeemer.

Mother of God. The title *Theotokos*, a Greek word meaning "God-bearer" or "Mother of God" was first applied to Mary in the early centuries of the church. The title acknowledged that Mary's child, Jesus, was truly God as well as man.

In the fourth century a bishop of Constantinople named Nestorius challenged the title. Nestorius wanted to call Mary only "Mother of Christ"; he feared that the title "Mother of God" would confuse the divine and human aspects of Jesus. The church in the East rose up to reject Nestorius' view. To deny that Mary was the mother of God was to deny either that Jesus is God or that Mary was truly his mother. A general council of bishops at Ephesus in 431 A.D. declared, "If anyone does not confess that God is truly Emmanuel, and that on this account the holy virgin is the mother of God (for according to the flesh she gave birth to the Word of God become flesh by birth), let him be anathema (condemned)."[12]

The council carefully stated that Mary is the mother of God "according to the flesh" to clarify that Mary is not the source of Jesus' divinity. Mary did not give birth to God in the beginning. But since the divine and human natures of Jesus are inseparable, Mary must be considered the mother of God as well as the mother of the man Jesus.

As the Catholic bishops of Canada have explained, "Mary conceived and gave birth not to a mere man, but to the person of the Son of God. To be sure, she did not conceive and give birth to his infinite divinity. She bore the Son of God in his humanity conceived from her flesh by the power of the Holy Spirit. Recognition and praise of Mary as Mother of God preserves the basic truth about the person and being of Jesus Christ as true God. This title also emphasizes his true humanity because he was truly born of a human mother."[13]

The Immaculate Conception. As Christians continued to reflect on who Jesus was and what it meant to be his mother, they came to a conviction that God had prepared a special place for Mary in his plan of redemption. This conviction was not easy to arrive at, because two factors appeared to conflict.

On the one hand, every human person is in need of God's redemption through Jesus Christ because of the fallen, sinful condition of mankind. As scripture says, "all have sinned and fall short of the glory of God and are justified freely by his grace through the redemption through Jesus Christ" (Rom 3:23-24). On the other hand, it seemed impossible to Christians that the all-holy God, whose very nature is opposed to sin, could have been born to someone bound by the sin and rebellion of the fallen human condition. How could Mary have been a sinner, and still have carried the fullness of the all-holy God in her womb? How could she have consented so freely and unquestioningly to God's plan if she shared the rebellious nature of the children of Adam and Eve?

Christians eventually came to believe that it would have been impossible for Mary to respond as she did, and for God to dwell within her, unless God had given her a remarkable, special grace. It was beyond the capacity of an ordinary human being to respond as Mary did and to have the fullness of God dwell within her without God's special assistance.

This special assistance or grace that enabled Mary to become the Mother of God is called Mary's "Immaculate Conception." It is the belief that arose among the early Christians that God had preserved Mary from the inheritance of original sin passed on to all mankind from our first parents. Mary did not have an extraordinary birth, as Jesus did: she had a normal human mother and father and was conceived and born in a normal way. The doctrine of the Immaculate Conception holds that Mary was preserved by God from original sin from the moment she was conceived. This was God's perfect act of purification to prepare Mary to bear the Son of God in her womb.

The doctrine of Mary's Immaculate Conception is more of a statement about Jesus than about Mary. It proclaims that Jesus was someone so unique and holy that God would even prepare his mother for his birth by preserving her from sin.

The belief in Mary's sinlessness appeared early in church history. In the fourth century St. Ambrose spoke of Mary as "free of every stain of sin."[14] St. Augustine believed that she was the one exception to the scripture text, "If we say we have not sinned, we deceive ourselves" (1 Jn 1:8). "For," Augustine argued, "how do we know what abundance of grace for the total overcoming of sin was conferred upon her, who merited to conceive and bear him in whom there was no sin?"[15] The Latin church resoundingly confirmed Augustine's insight, and the Eastern church had arrived at the same conclusion by the seventh century, exalting Mary's sinlessness as that of "a lily among thorns."[16]

However, some influential Catholic Christians expressed reservations about this doctrine, because it appeared to imply that Mary did not need Christ as her Savior. The church seemed to be caught in a dilemma: it did not seem correct that the mother of God was stained by sin, but it was necessary to believe that Mary had been redeemed from sin by Jesus Christ like everyone else. Even such a great figure as St. Thomas Aquinas could not fully accept the doctrine of the Immaculate Conception for this reason.

Fr. Raymond Brown, S.S., explains the solution the church finally reached:

> The objections of Aquinas and others were perfectly valid: Every human being needs the grace of Christ; if Mary was conceived without sin in such a way that she did not need the grace of Christ, that would be a denial of the Gospel. Duns Scotus was able to win the day because of his insight that the Immaculate Conception came through God's application of the grace of Christ beforehand. Our belief is that every human being through faith and through baptism is freed from sin through the grace of Christ. This is a basic privilege of disciples. We claim only that Mary was the first one to whom this was done; for according to God's plan, it was done even before she was conceived. Now this is an enormous privilege; still it does not move her over to the side of deity, but keeps her part of sanctified humanity. She was the first one to receive a basic consequence of discipleship that all Christians receive. That is harmonious with Luke's notion that she was the first Christian. I can see why Protestants might still say to us: We do not see why it had to happen in her case. But if I am right in emphasizing the line of development, non-Catholics cannot say to us: What you are saying is against the Gospel. Rather it is an application of the Gospel principle of Mary's unique place in discipleship.[17]

Therefore, as Catholic pastors and theologians looked more deeply into the objections to belief in the Immaculate Conception, they came to the conclusion that this doctrine does not contradict the Bible. The doctrine of the Immaculate Conception does not deny that all men need a redeemer. Mary too needed a redeemer and she was indeed saved from sin by the death and resurrection of her son Jesus. The Immaculate Conception means that the Lord applied the grace of Jesus' salvation to Mary in advance to prepare her for her special role in his plan. Why did the angel declare Mary to be "full of grace" (Lk 1:28), and Elizabeth proclaim her to be "blessed... among women" (Lk 1:42)? Because, as Mary said, "He who is mighty has done great things for me. Holy is his name!" (Lk 1:49)

As theological discussion dealt with the objections to the Immaculate Conception, the belief came to be almost universally held by Roman Catholics. Finally, in 1854, Pope Pius IX defined it as an official teaching of the Catholic Church in these words: "The Blessed Virgin Mary, in the first instant of her conception, by a singular grace and privilege of almighty God, and in view of the foreseen merits of Jesus Christ, the savior of the human race, was preserved free from all stain of original sin."[18] Pope Pius stressed that Mary's sinlessness was not due to her own merits, but that she was truly redeemed by the merits of her son Jesus.

Many Catholics believe that God provided a striking confirmation of this papal definition. Four years after Pius IX had declared that Mary was conceived without sin, on the Feast of the Annunciation in 1858, a beautiful Lady appeared to a simple peasant girl, Bernadette Soubirous, at Lourdes, France. The Lady told her, "I am the Immaculate Conception." At the time, Bernadette did not even know what "Immaculate Conception" meant, but repeated these words to a trusted friend.[19] Many Catholics believe that Bernadette had an authentic experience of Mary at Lourdes. Catholics are familiar with the many medically verified healings and other miracles that have occurred at Lourdes since 1858, through the intercession of Mary, the Immaculate Conception.

The Assumption of Mary. The Catholic belief in the "Assumption" of Mary into heaven is in some ways connected to her Immaculate Conception. The doctrine of the Assumption was officially defined on November 1, 1950, when Pope Pius XII declared that Mary, "having completed the course of her earthly life, was assumed body and soul to heavenly glory."[20] This means that at the end of Mary's time on earth, she experienced the "resurrection of the body" that is promised to all faithful followers of Jesus. Like the Immaculate Conception, the doctrine of the Assumption simply proclaims that Mary experienced in advance an aspect of salvation that is promised to all believers. The concept of the Immaculate Conception explains how Mary was saved from sin by Jesus in a unique way; Mary's Assumption shows the result of this freedom from sin—the immediate union of her whole being with God at the end of her life.

The book of Genesis implies that if Mary was preserved from sin by the free gift of God, she would not be bound to experience the consequences of sin—death—in the same way we do. Her Assumption into heaven might be understood as a sign of what might have happened at the end of all our lives had Adam and Eve not sinned.

Like the doctrine of the Immaculate Conception, the belief that Mary was taken bodily up to heaven emerged among early Christians and was almost unanimously accepted among Christians by the thirteenth century. The doctrine was finally defined as a Catholic belief by an "infallible" statement of Pope Pius XII in 1950 in response to the faith of millions of Catholics who desired that the Pope speak out officially about the truth of this belief. In the hundred years before Pope Pius' declaration, the popes had received petitions from 113 cardinals, 250 bishops, 32,000 priests and religious brothers, 50,000 religious women, and 8 million lay people, all requesting that the Assumption be recognized officially as a Catholic teaching. Apparently, the pope discerned that the Holy Spirit was speaking through the people of God on this matter.[21]

Belief in the Assumption is a source of hope for Christians because it foreshadows what will one day happen to each faithful Christian. The raising of Mary, body and soul, to the glory of heaven anticipates what will happen at the final judgment to all who are to be saved. It provides hope that Christians will one day experience the resurrection of the body that she has already experienced through the grace of her Son, Jesus Christ.

Devotion to Mary

In addition to understanding the most important Catholic doctrines about Mary, we need to examine Catholic devotion to her. How do Catholics relate to Mary in their day-to-day Christian lives?

Catholics do not worship Mary, but they do address Mary in prayer and ask her to pray and intercede to the Lord God on their behalf. Numerous Catholic prayers that are ultimately directed to God also address Mary and seek her protection, help, and intercession. Catholics pray this way because they believe that Mary continues to have a vital cooperative role in God's plan of salvation, just as she did when she accepted Jesus into her womb and eventually became his disciple. Now Mary is with the Lord, enjoying the glory and reward of faithful discipleship, and continuing to have a motherly concern and powerful role of intercession for all God's people.

Catholics also use physical reminders of Mary's role— statues, medals, scapulars, and rosaries. All of these objects are reminders of Mary's presence with God and of her role in his saving plan. They have no magical power to save. We are saved through Jesus Christ and are called to live a life committed to serving God and our neighbor, as Mary exemplified in her own life.

Because of their part in Catholic life, I will briefly discuss prayers addressing Mary, and especially the most important form of Marian prayer, the rosary.

The "Hail Mary". Devotion to Mary and prayer addressed to her is not a recent innovation. The earliest prayer of petition addressed to Mary that has come down to us dates from the latter part of the third century. The oldest text, which may well have been a cry for help in the days of the martyrs under Diocletian (303), is the following:

> We take refuge under the protection of your motherly mercy, O Mother of God. Despise not our fervent cries for help in the necessity in which we find ourselves. But deliver us from danger. Rescue us. Do not lead our plea into temptation, but deliver us from danger.

Among Catholics, the most common prayer addressed to Mary today is the "Hail Mary." It consists of three parts: the words of the Archangel Gabriel (Lk 1:28), "Hail (Mary) full of grace, the Lord is with thee, blessed are thou amongst women"; the words of Elizabeth under the inspiration of the Holy Spirit (Lk 1:42), "Blessed is the fruit of thy womb (Jesus)"; and a formula of petition, "Holy Mary, Mother of God, pray for us sinners now and at the hour of our death, Amen." The prayer is the result of a gradual development from the sixth century to the sixteenth, when the present wording was adopted. Originally, the prayer consisted only of the two-fold scriptural greeting of Mary, but because this seemed incomplete, an element of petition was added. The idea of petitioning Mary, asking her to pray for us, as we have seen dates back to at least the third century.

It is important to note that the "Hail Mary" is a scriptural prayer, and that the petition asks Mary to pray to the Lord for us, both now and when we die. Mary is honored as scripture honors her. She is not worshipped, but simply asked to pray for us.

The Rosary. Space does not permit an extensive study of the historical development of the rosary. The only question that will be considered here is whether the rosary is a legitimate Christian form of prayer. The rosary contains a number of different prayers: The Our Father (the Lord's Prayer), the Hail Mary, and a doxology of praise to the Trinity, the "Glory be to the Father." The rosary also begins with the sign of the cross and the Apostles' Creed. If the "Hail Mary" and the sign of the cross are viewed as legitimate Christian prayers, then the rosary as a whole should be accepted.

However, the rosary is more than just a recitation or repetition of individual prayers. It is meant to be a *meditation,* with Mary, on some of the central mysteries of Christianity. The rosary is divided into fifteen "decades," each devoted to meditation on one aspect or "mystery" of the life of Christ or Mary. The fifteen decades are actually subdivided into three sets of "mysteries":

> *The Sorrowful Mysteries:* Jesus' Agony in the Garden, Jesus' Scourging at the Pillar, Jesus' Crowning with Thorns, Jesus' Carrying of the Cross, Jesus' Crucifixion.

> *The Joyful Mysteries:* The Annunciation—Announcement to Mary of Jesus' Conception, The Visitation—Mary's visit to Elizabeth, The Birth of Jesus, The Presentation of Jesus in the Temple, The Finding of Jesus in the Temple (at age 12).

> *The Glorious Mysteries:* The Resurrection of Jesus, The Ascension of Jesus, The Descent of the Holy Spirit (Pentecost), The Assumption of Mary into Heaven, The Crowning of Mary as "Queen of Heaven."

When the rosary is said prayerfully, it is not a mindless repetition of rote prayers, but it is an occasion to reflect on these "mysteries of salvation." It is a fruitful form of contemplative or reflective prayer. Catholics also often use the rosary as a prayer of petition or intercession for specific needs or intentions.

Catholics affirm that the rosary is a Christian prayer. It is directed to the praise and glory of God, and it leads to deeper reflection on God's powerful works in the lives of Jesus and Mary. It also builds solidarity and unity in the body of Christ when it is prayed in a group or in pairs, or when it is offered in petition for the needs of God's people.

Yet the Rosary is not a required form of Catholic devotion. As Pope Paul VI noted in his apostolic exhortation on "Devotion to the Blessed Virgin Mary" (*Marialis Cultus*) on February 2, 1974:

> In concluding these observations, which give proof of the concern and esteem which the Apostolic See has for the Rosary of the Blessed Virgin, we desire at the same time to recommend that this very worthy devotion should not be propagated in a way that is too one-sided or exclusive. The Rosary is an excellent prayer, but the faithful should feel serenely free in its regard. They should be drawn to its calm recitation by its intrinsic appeal.[22]

Appearances of Mary

What do Catholic Christians believe about the many reported appearances or "apparitions" of Mary that have occurred throughout Christian history, and which seem to have been especially frequent in the past 150 years? First, such apparitions are private revelations, distinguished from the official public revelation of the Bible and the authentic apostolic tradition. Pope John Paul II spoke of the relationship between these two forms of revelation in a homily at Fatima on May 13, 1982:

> The Church has always taught and continues to proclaim that God's revelation was brought to completion in Jesus Christ, who is the fullness of that revelation, and that "no new public revelation is to be expected before the glorious

manifestation of the Lord" (Dogmatic Constitution on Divine Revelation, no. 4). The Church evaluates and judges private revelations by the criterion of conformity with that single public revelation.[23]

Therefore, private revelations such as appearances of Mary must conform fully to the standard of public revelation that comes from Jesus Christ. Further, the Catholic Church does not require its members to believe in or to accept the validity of any particular private revelation.

However, Catholic Christians realize that God has not ceased to guide and reveal himself to his people in many ways through the centuries. In Old Testament times, God often spoke to his people through messengers, such as angels and prophets. Many Catholics find the evidence convincing that God has often sent Mary, in these New Testament times, to convey significant messages. If God could convey messages through angels, why could he not send Mary, the servant of the Lord, to speak to man and reveal his will?

Fr. John Bertolucci has noted that the reported appearances or "visitations" of Mary in recent times have followed a biblical pattern. They always have been made to simple, humble and usually poor people; they have been accompanied by an outpouring of the Holy Spirit; they have stirred up a deep trust in God, even in the midst of oppression; and they have produced a rich harvest of "good fruit," including joy, thanksgiving and an outburst of worship and praise of God. Healings and other miracles have accompanied such apparitions, further confirming their validity and importance.[24]

Even though appearances of Mary are not a central part of Catholic belief, many Catholics believe that Mary has an important prophetic and evangelistic mission in our times. Some of the reported appearances of Mary in the past have had a profound effect on the lives of millions of people. About 450 years ago, Mary appeared to Juan Diego, a Mexican peasant. She was garbed in the robes of one of the poor and oppressed native Indian tribes of the area. This appearance of "Our Lady of Guadalupe" gave the Indians hope and a belief in God's care for them. Within seven years about eight million native Indians were baptized as Christians. "Our Lady of Guadalupe" became the patroness of Mexico. Many Catholics firmly believed that God had sent Mary on a crucial evangelistic mission, speaking the gospel message of hope and good news for the poor.[25]

The main message of the appearance of Mary at Lourdes, France in 1858 to fourteen-year-old Bernadette Soubirous was Mary herself. God presented the Immaculate Conception as a model of holiness who reflects the grace and holiness of the church. Thousands of people who have visited Lourdes have been healed and turned to Jesus Christ.

Perhaps the most striking appearances of Mary in our time occurred at Fatima, Portugal in 1917. Mary appeared to three children, aged seven to ten, and presented a disturbing message about the perilous situation of the world and the dire consequences in store if mankind did not repent and turn to God. Mary revealed that the destiny of both individuals and nations hinged on whether people prayed and interceded for salvation. In particular, Mary asked for the consecration of Russia to her immaculate heart. She warned, "If my requests are heard, Russia will be converted and there will be peace. If not, she will spread her errors throughout the entire world, provoking wars and persecution of the Church...."[26] At that time, Russia was a poor country torn by civil war, and this prediction seemed almost laughable. But history has proven it true. Mary's appearance at Fatima reminds Christians that the things we do now and our prayers and faith have consequences for our own salvation and for that of the world. As Pope John Paul II stated in his homily at Fatima on May 13, 1982:

> If the church has accepted the message of Fatima, it is above all because that message contains a truth and a call whose basic content is the truth and call of the gospel itself.

"Repent, and believe in the Gospel" (Mk 1:15): these are the first words that the Messiah addressed to humanity. The message of Fatima is, in its basic nucleus, a call to conversion and repentance, as in the Gospel. . . .

At Fatima, Mary promised a sign of the validity and truth of her appearances there. It is estimated that about 100,000 people witnessed this sign—the sun dancing in the sky at mid-day. Many secular observers witnessed this sign, and have not been able to explain it. It has often been ignored, but never effectively denied.[27]

There are many more reported appearances of Mary. The Catholic Church has always been wary about placing undue emphasis on these private revelations, but many of them have been accepted as legitimate by the local bishops, whose role it is to discern their validity. In the most widely accepted apparitions, Mary has consistently called Christians to prayer, repentance, and conversion to God. Sometimes she has warned of serious consequences for the world if this message remains unheeded. Mary always has presented herself in authentic apparitions as a messenger or servant of God. Although she has affirmed traditional Catholic titles for herself and encouraged the use of "Marian" prayers, such as the rosary, her focus is always unmistakably centered on Jesus Christ. The most recent appearances of Mary, In Medjugorge, Yugoslavia, repeat many of the themes of the message of Mary at Fatima, and affirm the basic truths of the gospel and Catholic Christian teaching.

Although the Catholic Church does not insist upon belief in these appearances of Mary, they are happenings that Christians should prayerfully consider. If God is speaking a prophetic word to the church today through Mary, Christians at least ought to be willing to listen to her message in order to test it. If God does continue to speak to the world through Mary, this could be another sign to Christians of her continuing role in his plan of salvation.

Mary and Us

What place does Mary have in the actual life and beliefs of a Christian? It is all too easy to say, "No place," or "Very little," for fear of detracting from the love and worship of God. Certainly Christians must always place God above all else. And yet we might also imagine ourselves as the "beloved disciple" at the foot of the cross to whom Jesus said, "Behold, your mother." Jesus seemed to think that his beloved disciples could find a place in their hearts for a relationship with Mary as their mother, and could accept her maternal love and care. Her role in the Christian life certainly does not compete with the role of Jesus. Fr. Francis Martin once observed that anyone who confuses the roles of Mary and Jesus does not have a problem with their "Mariology"; their problem is that they have never really met Jesus Christ. Those who really know the life and power of Jesus will never be tempted or able to confuse Jesus' role with that of Mary.[28]

Another obstacle to approaching Mary is the fact that she is sometimes presented as being super-human or even divine. With all the special graces and privileges that Catholics believe God gave to Mary, it would be easy to think of her as abnormal or as some sort of goddess.

Mary is special, in that she alone was chosen by God to be the "ark of the new covenant" by which God entered fully into our world. Only Mary was the mother of God, conceiving her son by the Holy Spirit and yet remaining a virgin.

On the other hand, Mary is really more normal than any of us, if by "normal" we mean closer to what God originally intended human beings to be. God did not will sin and death for mankind. He preserved Mary from these things to remind us what normal human life is really meant to be.

Mary was also normal in that she was not spared the trials and sufferings of this life that have come as a result of sin. If anything, she experienced the horror of sin even more acutely because of the special grace God had given her. Because she bore the cross of Jesus so fully in this life, she is now experiencing a unique fullness of his glory in heaven.

TEN

Man's Destiny in Christ

OUR LIFE ON EARTH is a fleeting moment, a preparation for eternal life and "the things to come"—heaven, hell, death, judgment, and the second coming of Christ. Christians should not be fearful or anxious in confronting these last things. Jesus Christ has conquered sin and death, and has revealed the truth about the eternal destiny of mankind. As the apostle Paul wrote:

Death is swallowed up in victory. O death, where is your victory? O death where is your sting? The sting of death is sin, and the power of sin is the law. But thanks be to God who gives us the victory through our Lord Jesus Christ.

Therefore, my beloved brethren, be steadfast, immovable, always abounding in the work of the Lord, knowing that in the Lord your labor is not in vain. (1 Cor 15:54-58)

Christians look forward to death and the "end times" with hope. Through Jesus Christ, the end times will be times of victory for God's faithful people.

Heaven

Heaven is eternal life with God. It is the goal of human existence, the purpose for which God created all mankind. The account of the Fall in Genesis reveals that God's original plan was to unite all of mankind with him in everlasting life. Man's sin disrupted this plan. He became subject to physical death and to hell—the ultimate death of eternal separation from God. Yet God mercifully restored his plan of life for mankind through his Son, Jesus Christ. As the gospel of John tells us, "God so loved the world that he gave his only Son, that whoever believes in him should not perish, but have eternal life" (Jn 3:16). Paul emphasizes that God's love and desire for salvation extends to *all* mankind, for God

> desires all men to be saved and to come to the knowledge of the truth. For there is one God, and there is one mediator between God and men, the man Jesus Christ, who gave himself as a ransom for all . . . we have our hope set on the living God, who is the Savior of all men, especially of those who believe. (1 Tm 2:4-6, 4:10)

Jesus Christ is the Son of God, the one mediator between God and men, and the "first-born" of a new creation (see Col 1:15-20), the founder of a new race of men and women who are no longer destined to die, but who will live eternally with God in heaven.

What will heaven be like? The New Testament describes it as a joyous wedding feast (Mt 22:1-14, 25:1-13) and a great banquet (Lk 14:16-24) that will last forever. The book of Revelation describes heaven as the marriage of the Lamb, Jesus Christ, to his Bride, the church (Rv 19:7-9). The ultimate glory of heaven will be the joy of seeing God and being perfectly transformed into his image. "Now we see indistinctly as in a mirror; then we shall see face to face. My knowledge is imperfect now; then I shall know even as I am known" (1 Cor 13:12). Catholics traditionally have called this face-to-face encounter with God in heaven the "beatific vision," the vision of God that brings perfect happiness.

The truth contained in these biblical images is clear. Heaven is real, and some human beings will live forever in the joy of God's presence.

Who will attain the life of heaven? How many people will be there? Catholic Christians believe that God does not satisfy our curiosity about such questions. The book of Revelation speaks of 144,000 elect, but this is a symbolic figure suggesting the perfect number (12 times 12 times 1,000). Rather than speculating about who or how many will be in heaven, we should follow the exhortation of Jesus: "strive to enter by the narrow door; for many, I tell you, will seek to enter and will not be able" (Lk 13:24). Or as Paul urged, seek "to work out your own salvation with fear and trembling; for God is at work in you, both to will and to work for his good pleasure" (Phil 2:12-13).

Hell

God desires that all people be saved, but Jesus clearly warned that not everyone will be: "Enter by the narrow gate; for the gate is wide and the way is easy that leads to destruction, and those who enter it are many. For the gate is narrow and the way is hard that leads to life, and those who find it are few." (Mt 7:13-14) In the parables in which Jesus compared heaven to a wedding feast, a banquet, and a harvest, he also stressed that not everyone will be invited or gathered into the fulfilled kingdom. Some will be expelled to the outer darkness, where men will "weep and gnash their teeth" (Mt 22:13, 24:51, 25:30). There the "chaff" will be burned with "unquenchable fire" (Lk 3:17; Mt 3:12, 13:30), "where the worm does not die, and the fire is not quenched" (Mk 9:48).

These are the images of what the Bible calls "hell" (Mk 9:46, 47; Mt 18:9), the state of eternal punishment and separation from God. Jesus clearly taught that hell was real (see Lk 16:19-31; Mt 18:7-9), and implied that many people will end up there (see Mt 7:13-14, 24:40-41).

Hell is an unpopular concept today, and some modern theologians question its existence or suggest that very few people will actually go there. The teaching of the Roman Catholic Church, however, is that hell does exist and that those who refuse to believe in Jesus, or who live in opposition to God and his will, will be condemned there in eternal separation from God. The apostle Paul warned against those who so emphasized the mercy and love of God that they neglected his justice in punishing those who refused to repent:

> Or do you presume upon the riches of his kindness and forbearance and patience? Do you not know that God's kindness is meant to lead you to repentance? But by your hard and impenitent heart you are storing up wrath for yourself on the day of wrath when God's righteous judgment will be revealed. For he will render to every man according to his works: to those who by patience in well-doing seek for glory and honor and immortality he will give eternal life, but for those who are factious and do not obey the truth, but obey wickedness, there will be wrath and fury.
> (Rom 2:4-8)

As with heaven, we do not fully comprehend what hell will be like, but all of the biblical images suggest that it is a place of darkness and torment (see Mt 25:30; Lk 16:28), fire (see Mt 18:9, 13:30), wrath and fury (see Rom 2:8). Hell is not a place anyone would wish to go, much less spend eternity! Perhaps the greatest pain of those who are condemned to hell is their hopeless awareness that they are forever separated from God, and their knowledge that they are fully responsible for having brought this fate upon themselves. For as John's gospel makes clear, Jesus did not come to condemn, but to save. Those who freely reject Jesus and his word condemn themselves by their own free decisions (see Jn 3:17-21, 12:47-48; Lk 19:10; Mt 12:36-37).

Purgatory

Scripture and Christian tradition undoubtedly affirm that heaven and hell exist, but what about that mysterious "third state" that Catholics and some other Christians call "purgatory?" The term itself is not found in the Bible but the same may be said of other important Christian doctrines, such as the terms "Trinity" and "Incarnation."

God is constantly at work throughout our lives to purge us of sin. Catholics believe that God completes this purifying work after a person's death for those whose lives on earth basically have been oriented toward God and his will. Purgatory is not a second chance for salvation for those who have rejected God or have lived evil lives. Neither is it a safety net for people who hope that God will overlook serious sin in their lives if they die unrepentant. Rather, purgatory is a sign of God's mercy on those who have honestly sought to know God and to do his will in this life, and yet who die in some degree of bondage to sin or the effects of sin. God hates sin, and he would be perfectly just in condemning to hell all those bound by even the slightest sin or sin's effects at the time of their death. Instead, Catholics believe that God chooses to purify repentant sinners even after their death so that they can enter into the full joy of heaven.

But why is this necessary? Why do people need to be purified or purged of sin after they die? Don't the merits of Jesus Christ's death suffice for the total remission of sin?

The answer to this last question is "yes," all sin is totally forgiven and removed through the passion, death, and resurrection of Jesus Christ. Catholic Christians understand purgatory as a way that this salvation in Jesus actually "happens" or is applied to individual persons. If a person dies in some bondage to sin, or has been crippled by sin's effects, this sin and its effects must be removed, forgiven, and purged before the person sees God face-to-face. Why? Because of God's *holiness*.

Sin and God are diametrically opposed. God is so pure, so holy, that nothing impure or sinful can enter into his presence (see Rv 21:27). Sin is burned away by God's holiness, by his anger against sin, and by his love of the repentant sinner, "for our God is a consuming fire" (Heb 12:29). Purgatory means that as a person is drawn nearer to God and finally drawn into the full glory of his presence, the remaining sin in a person's life is just burned away by the consuming fire of God's hatred of sin and his love for one bound by it. Sin is purged because it cannot exist in the presence of the all-holy God.

This understanding of God's holiness and the purging from sin is indicated in some biblical texts. The Hebrew people of the Old Covenant knew God's awesome holiness, and believed that if a person were to come directly into God's presence, he would die. Moses boldly asked God to "show me your glory." But God told Moses, "you cannot see my face; for man shall not see me and live" (Ex 33:20). God then hid Moses in the cleft of a rock, and allowed Moses to see only his "back" after he passed by.

The prophet Isaiah had a vision of God upon a throne with the angels surrounding him crying, "Holy, holy, holy, is the Lord of hosts" (Is 6:1-3). Isaiah's immediate response was: "Woe is me! For I am a man of unclean lips...yet my eyes have seen...the Lord of hosts!" (Is 6:5). But the Lord sent an angel to purify Isaiah's lips with a burning coal from the altar of God. "And he touched my mouth and said, "Behold, this has touched your lips; your guilt is taken away and your sin forgiven" (Is 6:7). Only then was Isaiah able to speak the Word of God to the people.

The doctrine of purgatory is related to Isaiah's experience. When people come before God in reality (not just in a vision), they will see their sin as it really is, ugly and detestable, and cry out, "Woe is me!" But for those whose lives have been spent in seeking God and striving to do his will, God in his mercy will send the fire of his love to purify them from that sin, so they can stand before him joyfully to praise God forever.

Catholic Christians believe that the New Testament also affirms the reality of purgatory. In 1 Cor 3:11-15, Paul writes:

> For no other foundation can one lay than that which is laid, which is Jesus Christ. Now if anyone builds on the foundation with gold, silver, precious stones, wood, hay, stubble, each man's work will become manifest, for the Day will disclose it, because it will be revealed with fire, and the fire will test what sort of work each one has done. If the work which any has built on the foundation survives, he will receive a reward. If any man's work is burned up, he will suffer loss, though he himself will be saved, but only as through fire (1 Cor 3:11-15).

This passage speaks about those who have built their lives on the foundation of Jesus Christ. When these people are judged, the "work" they have done in this life will be tested. If it is good, they will be rewarded. If their work is inferior (sinful), the fire of judgment will burn it up. These people will "suffer loss," although they will be saved "but only as through fire." Christians in the early church who reflected on this passage came to believe that a "purification by fire"—a purgatory—would come upon those Christians whose lives and works were imperfect in God's sight, although they themselves would be saved. The image of fire connected with purgatory shows that this "purgation" is painful, yet also cleansing and purifying. This is not an unfamiliar idea; even in this life we experience pain when God breaks us from patterns of sin, although this is a healing and liberating work.

The belief in purgatory is also supported in the ancient Christian practice of praying for the dead. Very early, Christians began to honor and pray for their deceased relatives and friends. Inscriptions in the Roman catacombs indicate that some of the earliest Christians did this. Around 211 A.D., Tertullian wrote that Christians offered prayer and the Eucharist for the deceased on the anniversaries of their death.[1]

The list of the great "fathers" of the early church who encouraged Christians to pray for the dead is impressive: Tertullian, Origen, Cyprian, Ambrose, Augustine, Basil, Gregory of Nazianzus, John Chrysostom, Pope Gregory the Great, and many others. Gregory of Nyssa wrote that "after the departure from the body (a soul that is not purified)... will not be able to participate in divinity, unless the cleansing fire will have purged away all stains on the soul." The ancient liturgies of the church included powerful prayers for the dead, such as the beginning of this prayer from the liturgy of St. John Chrysostom: "Let us pray also for the repose of the souls of the departed servants of God and for the forgiveness of their every transgression, deliberate and indeliberate...."[2]

Praying for the dead makes sense only if those prayers can benefit the dead. If they had already arrived at their final eternal destiny, heaven or hell, then praying for the dead would be futile. However, if the deceased were undergoing the healing and purification of purgatory, then prayer for God's mercy on them would be reasonable and fitting.

Prayer for the dead became a common practice in the early church because the early Christians believed that the Holy Spirit had led them to do this, based on this understanding of man's destiny after death. The early Christians believed that their prayers could hasten God's work of purifying and purging their deceased relatives and friends from sin by calling upon his mercy. Catholic Christians have held this belief from the earliest times of Christianity until today. The Second Vatican Council taught:

> Very much aware of the bonds linking the whole Mystical Body of Jesus Christ, the pilgrim Church from the very first ages of the Christian religion has cultivated with great piety the memory of the dead. Because it is "a holy and wholesome thought to pray for the dead that they may be loosed from sin (2 Mc 12:46), she has also offered prayers for them.[3]

The Second Coming of Christ

Catholic Christians believe that purgatory is a temporary state. When the Lord Jesus comes again in majesty, purgatory will come to an end, as will life on earth as we know it now. The purification of those in purgatory and on earth will be completed in the last judgment of the living and the dead. Then only two states will remain: heaven and hell.

The Bible and Christian tradition have given many names to the time when the glorified Jesus will return to judge mankind and to bring human history to a close—the day of the Lord, the parousia, the end-time, and the second coming of Christ. Some Christians believe that the second coming will inaugurate a thousand year reign of Christ on earth, often called the "millenium," mentioned in the book of Revelation (Ch. 19 and 20).

Catholic Christians have usually followed St. Augustine's interpretation of this text. To him, the thousand years (which is a biblical way of saying "a very long time") represents the whole history of the church—from the sending of the Holy Spirit at Pentecost until Christ's return at the end of time. It is a time of God's victory, but also a time of conflict. Jesus Christ has won the victory by his death on the cross, and yet Satan and his demons are still at work in the world, warring against the church. As this period of history closes, Satan's power will increase until Jesus comes to earth again and condemns him and his followers to eternity in hell, or the "lake of fire" (Rv 20:10-14). Followers of Jesus, whose names are written in the "book of life," will then enter forever into the "new Jerusalem" of heaven (see Rv 21).[4]

What will the second coming of Christ be like? The Catholic Church has always affirmed and proclaimed certain biblical truths about the second coming of Jesus. The first basic truth is that Jesus will return to earth as the glorified "Son of Man" (see Dn 7:13, 14) to judge mankind and bring human history to an end (see Mk 13:26-27; Mt 25:31-46; Acts 1:11; 1 Thes

4:16-17; 1 Cor 15:22-23; Jas 5:7-9; 2 Tm 4:8). Nearly all of these biblical texts use bold, vivid images, called "apocalyptic" or "revelational" images, to describe the second coming. For example, in 1 Thes 4:16-17 Paul speaks of archangel voices, the "trumpet of God," and people "caught up . . . in the clouds to meet the Lord in the air," an event some Christians call the "rapture."

Are these apocalyptic images literal descriptions of what the second coming of Christ will be like, or are they vivid images created by the Hebrew people to imagine what the parousia could be like? Many biblical scholars confidently affirm that these are poetic images not to be taken as a literal description of the "end-times." Many Christians firmly believe that these images are a literal description of the second coming of Jesus. To my knowledge, the Catholic Church has never made any official statement on this question. This is wise, because no one will know whether the biblical images are poetic or literal until the second coming actually happens. Rather than becoming entangled in arguments about this point, Catholic Christians prefer to focus on the basic truths contained in these passages that everyone can agree on. The first basic truth is that Jesus will return to earth as the glorious Son of Man to bring human history to an end and to judge all mankind. Catholic Christians profess in the creed, "He will come again in glory to judge the living and the dead," and proclaim in the Mass, "Christ has died, Christ is risen, Christ will come again!"

The second basic truth, related to the first, is that the second coming of Christ will be unmistakable because it will be accompanied by unprecedented signs in the heavens and on earth. "For as the lightning comes from the east and shines as far as the west, so will be the coming of the Son of Man" (Mt 24:27). Many people have "fallen for" false messiahs (saviors) and prophets over the centuries, and continue to do so today. But Catholic Christians believe that Jesus is the only Lord, the only Messiah, the only Savior, and that his coming again to earth will be clear and unmistakable.

The Bible indicates that certain "signs" will precede the parousia, and they fall roughly into two categories. The first are certain preliminary events that will occur sometime before Jesus' coming again. Paul, in his letter to the Romans (Rom 11:25-32) speaks of the conversion of Israel to Christ after the "full number" of Gentiles has been converted. And Mt 24:14 teaches: "And this gospel of the kingdom will be preached throughout the whole world, as a testimony to all the nations and then the end will come." These passages have been interpreted in various ways by both Catholic and Protestant scripture scholars, but most agree that they refer to significant events that will precede the second coming of Christ.

The second category of those "signs" are *proximate* signs, using the vivid apocalyptic images drawn from the Old Testament and other ancient literature. They are found especially in Mark 13, Matthew 24, and Luke 21. For example, the Synoptic gospels report that there will be a period of great tribulation or trial immediately before Christ's return. This trial will be characterized by confusion and disorder in the world, in the church, and even in the physical condition of the earth and the "heavens." Many will depart from the true Christian faith (1 Tm 4:1-2), and will lead increasingly self-centered and debauched lives (2 Tm 3:1-8), causing the love of many people to grow cold (Mt 24:12). The Bible also tells of the rise of an "anti-Christ," an evil person or power trying to destroy the work of God on earth and the reign of Jesus Christ (1 Jn 2:18-23, 4:1-5; Rv 20:7-8; 2 Thes 2:3-10).

There is little official Catholic teaching about how to understand these signs because the Catholic Church wants people to avoid pointless speculation about the identity of the anti-Christ and the nature of the tribulation. However, the Catholic Church encourages people to take seriously the basic teaching of the Bible. Christians should expect a time of extreme difficulty immediately before the glorious coming of Jesus Christ, accompanied by unprecedented signs of this coming in the heavens and on earth. The darkness of this world will grow even darker for those who have not acknowledged and believed in the Light and Savior of the world, Jesus Christ. However, there also will be signs of the light of Christ shining more brightly in the world as the gospel is proclaimed to all the nations, and as many Gentiles and Jews are converted to Christ.

The third basic truth about the second coming of Christ is that no one knows exactly when it will happen. It will be sudden and unexpected, catching many people unprepared. The time of Jesus' return is not ours to know. Many Christians today disagree with this statement and, like many Christians throughout the centuries, attempt to predict the time of Jesus' return.

Jesus himself said that even he did not know the exact time of his second coming: "But of that day or that hour no one knows, not even the angels in heaven, nor the Son, but only the Father" (Mk 13:32). Nearly every biblical scholar today believes this is an actual saying of Jesus himself because it is one of the rare times in the gospels in which Jesus claims to be ignorant of something. The gospel writers would certainly not have conceded that Jesus didn't know something, unless he actually claimed that he didn't.

Further, the parables of Jesus emphasize that the coming of the Lord will be sudden and unexpected. Matthew's gospel (24:36-25:12) records four consecutive parables in which Jesus warns his followers about how unexpected his coming again will be. A favorite biblical image for the exact time of Jesus' coming is that it will come like a "thief"—Paul uses it in 1 Thes 5:2; Peter uses it in 2 Pt 3:10; and it is also in Matthew's gospel (Mt 24:43). The point, of course, is that just as no one knows when a thief will break in, no one knows exactly when Christ will come again. Hence, Catholic Christians do not claim to know any more than Jesus or the Bible on this topic, and avoid speculating about how or when the end will come.

A fourth truth about the second coming is that Christians always should be prepared for it, and looking forward to it with expectation. In Mark's gospel, immediately after Jesus denied knowledge of the time of his second coming, he taught:

> Take heed, watch and pray, for you do not know when the time will come. . . . Watch, therefore, for you do not know when the master of the house will come, in the evening or at midnight, or at the cockcrow, or in the morning—lest he come suddenly and find you asleep. And what I say to you I say to all—Watch! (Mk 13:33, 35-37)

How do Christians watch for the second coming of the Lord? First, they are to prepare for his coming by leading holy and upright lives. Peter insisted on this in his two letters:

> Therefore, gird up your minds; be sober, set your hope fully upon the grace that is coming to you at the revelation of Jesus Christ. As obedient children, do not be conformed to the passions of your former ignorance, but as he who called you is holy, be holy yourselves in all your conduct.
>
> (1 Pt 1:13-15)

This point must not be overlooked, dear friends. In the Lord's eyes, one day is as a thousand years and a thousand years is as a day. The Lord does not delay in keeping his promise—though some consider it "delay." Rather, he shows you a generous patience, since he wants none to perish but all to come to repentance.

The day of the Lord will come as a thief, and on that day, the heavens will vanish with a roar; the elements will be destroyed by fire, and the earth and its deeds will be made manifest.

Since everything is to be destroyed in this way, what sort

of men must you not be! How holy is your conduct and devotion, looking for the coming of the day of God and trying to hasten it! (2 Pt 3:8-12)

One way to hasten the coming of the Lord is to pray for it. This is a second attitude that Christians should have toward the parousia. One of the oldest Christian prayers is "Maranatha"—"Come, Lord!"—a prayer begging the Lord Jesus to return soon to establish the fullness of his kingdom.

The third way that Christians should approach the second coming of Jesus Christ is to look forward to it with joyous expectation. The second coming is a time of glory and reward for all of Jesus' faithful followers. "God is not unjust; he will not forget your work and the love you have shown him by your service, past and present, to his holy people" (Heb 6:10). St. Paul wrote these words of encouragement to the Christians in Thessalonica:

> You are not in the dark, brothers, that the day [of Christ's coming] should catch you off guard, like a thief. No, all of you are children of light and of the day. We belong neither to darkness or to the night; therefore, let us not be asleep like the rest, but awake and sober! ... God has not destined us for wrath but for acquiring salvation through our Lord Jesus Christ. He died for us, that all of us, whether awake or asleep, together might live with him. (1 Thes 5:5-6, 9-10).

Christians who have believed in Christ and who have lived their lives in the light of his presence should have no fear of the day of judgment. As long as we do not fall into the darkness of sin, we have a confident hope of salvation. Jesus himself instructed his disciples, "now when these things [the signs immediately preceding his second coming] take place, look up and raise your heads, because your redemption is drawing near" (Lk 21:28).

Catholics are Christians and can look forward with confidence to obtaining eternal life with God, through the merits of the death and resurrection of Jesus Christ our Savior, and by the power of the Holy Spirit. Catholic Christians realize, with St. Paul, that

> this slight momentary affliction is preparing for us an eternal weight of glory beyond all comparison, because we look not to the things that are seen, but to the things that are unseen. For the things that are seen are transient, but the things that are unseen are eternal. (2 Cor 4:17-18)

> Therefore let us be grateful for receiving a kingdom that cannot be shaken, and let us offer to God acceptable worship, with reverence and awe; for our God is a consuming fire. (Heb 12:28-29)

MARANATHA! COME, LORD JESUS!

Notes

Introduction

1. Ralph Martin, *A Crisis of Truth* (Ann Arbor: Mich.: Servant, 1981).
2. Steve Clark, "Orthodox, Protestants, Roman Catholics: What Basis for Cooperation?" in *Summons to Faith and Renewal: Christian Renewal in a Post-Christian World* (Ann Arbor, Mich.: Servant, 1983), p. 101.

Prologue
Perspective on Catholic Beliefs

1. C.S. Lewis, *Mere Christianity* (New York: MacMillan Paperbacks, 1960), p. 46.
2. "Decree on Ecumenism," no. 11.
3. Nowhere does the Catholic Church present a formal list of this "hierarchy" and what truths are more important than others. However, a study of Catholic doctrine reveals that some truths have been consistently repeated and defended by the Catholic Church from the early centuries of Christianity until this day. Usually, these truths are more central to Christian faith.
4. "Protestants, Pentecostals, and Mary," Kilian McDonnell, *New Covenant,* March 1977, pp. 28, 29.

Chapter One
Salvation: God's Free Gift in Jesus Christ

1. Catholic teaching has always affirmed the existence of Satan. Pope Paul VI addressed this issue in a general audience given on November 15, 1973:

> What are the greatest needs of the Church today? Do not let our answer surprise you as being over-simple or even superstitious and unreal: one of the greatest needs is defense from that evil which is called the Devil. . . .
> . . . it is not a question of one Devil, but of many, (as) is indicated by various passages in the gospel (Lk 11:21; Mk 5:9). But the princpal one is Satan, which means the Adversary, the Enemy. . . .
> So we know that this dark and disturbing spirit really exists, and

that he still acts with treacherous cunning; he is the secret enemy that sows errors and misfortunes in human history. . . .

The question of the Devil and the influence he can exert on individual persons as well as on communities, whole societies, is a very important chapter of Catholic doctrine which is given little attention today, though it should be studied again. . . ." (Pope Paul VI, "Satan and the Catholic Tradition," *New Covenant,* April 1974, p. 8)

2. While modern biblical scholarship has indicated that the Catholic understanding of original sin cannot rest on this text alone (Rom 5:12), Catholic Christians still believe that the Bible as a whole supports the traditional interpretation that all mankind has become subject to sin and death through the "original sin"of Adam and Eve (see Gn 3, especially 3:23-24). "Original sin" is a formally defined doctrine of the Catholic Church. See the Council of Trent, "Decree on Original Sin," session V, 1546.

3. Second Vatican Council, "Dogmatic Constitution on the Church" (*Lumen Gentium*), no. 14.

4. Second Vatican Council, "Declaration on the Relationship of the Church to Non-Christian Religions," no. 4.

5. Second Vatican Council, "Decree on the Missionary Activity of the Church," no. 6, 7.

6. Second Vatican Council, "Message to Humanity," *The Documents of Vatican II,* Walter Abbott, S.J., ed. (New York: America Press, 1966), p. 4.

7. Second Vatican Council, "Decree on the Missionary Activity of the Church," no. 7.

8. Second Vatican Council, "Constitution on Divine Revelation," no. 5.

9. Second Vatican Council, "Decree on the Apostolate of the Laity," no. 6.

10. Council of Trent, "Decree on Justification," chap. 8.

11. Ibid.

12. Ibid.

13. Council of Trent, "Decree on Justification," chap. 16.

14. St. Cyprian of Carthage, "On the Unity of the Catholic Church," par. 6; Letter to Quintus, a bishop in Mauretania, 73, 21, quoted in *The Faith of the Early Fathers,* vol. 1, W.A. Jurgens, ed. (Collegeville, Minn.: Liturgical Press, 1970), pp. 221, 238.

15. St. Augustine of Hippo, *City of God,* Book XIX, chaps. 14-17, quoted in *Documents in Early Christian Thought,* Maurice Wiles and Mark Santer, eds., (London: Cambridge University Press, 1975), pp. 239-44.

16. Second Vatican Council, "Dogmatic Constitution on the Church," no. 14.

17. Council of Trent, "Decree on Justification," chap. 13.

Chapter Two
Where Do Catholic Beliefs Come From?

1. Second Vatican Council, "Dogmatic Constitution on Divine

Revelation," no. 11.
2. Clement of Rome, "The Letter of the Church of Rome to the Church of Corinth," commonly called "Clement's First Letter," in *Early Christian Fathers,* Cyril Richardson, ed. (New York: Macmillan, 1970) pp. 33-73.
3. Clement of Rome, "Clement's First Letter," 42:4-5. Richardson, p. 62.
4. Clement of Rome, "Clement's First Letter," 44:2. Richardson, p. 62.
5. Ignatius of Antioch, "Letter of Ignatius of Antioch to the Trallians," 2:1-2, quoted in Richardson, pp. 98-99.
6. Irenaeus of Lyons, "The Refutation and Overthrow of Knowledge Falsely So-Called" (Against Heresies), book III, 3, 1, quoted in Richardson, p. 371.
7. Ibid., book III, 3, 2, Richardson, p. 372.
8. Ibid.
9. "The three-tiered system of one bishop in one city, with presbyters and deacons, was attained in the second century without controversy." Henry Chadwick, *The Early Church* (London: Penguin Books, 1967), p. 51.
10. Henry Chadwick, *The Early Church,* p. 81.
11. Ibid., pp. 43, 44.
12. Eusebius, *History of the Church,* book III, chap. 25.
13. Second Vatican Council, "Dogmatic Constitution on Divine Revelation," no. 4.
14. Second Vatican Council, "Dogmatic Constitution on Divine Revelation," no. 9 and 10.

Chapter Three
The Church: How Catholics Understand It

1. Second Vatican Council, "Dogmatic Constitution on the Church," no. 9.
2. Ignatius of Antioch, Letter to the Smyrneans, 8:2, quoted in *Early Christian Fathers,* Cyril Richardson, ed., p. 115.
3. Augustine of Hippo, *Confessions,* book IX, chap. 10.
4. Eusebius of Caesarea, *History of the Church,* book IX, chaps. 9 and 11, Book X, chaps. 1, 2, 8, 9.
5. Second Vatican Council, "Decree on Ecumenism," no. 3.
6. Ibid., no. 1.
7. Ibid., no. 7.
8. Ibid., no 1.
9. Ibid., no. 3.
10. Second Vatican Council, "Dogmatic Constitution on the Church," no. 8.
11. Ibid., no. 15.
12. Ibid., no. 8.
13. Second Vatican Council, "The Decree on Ecumenism," no. 3.
14. Samuel McCrea Cavert, in *The Documents of Vatican II,* Walter Abbott, S.J., ed., p. 367.
15. Kilian McDonnell, O.S.B., *The Charismatic Renewal and Ecumenism*

(New York: Paulist Press), pp. 73-74.
16. Second Vatican Council, "Decree on Ecumenism," no. 24.
17. Ibid., no. 3.
18. Ibid., no. 4.
19. Ibid., no. 4.
20. Second Vatican Council, "Dogmatic Constitution on the Church," no. 8.
21. Second Vatican Council, "Decree on Ecumenism," no. 6.
22. Second Vatican Council, "Dogmatic Constitution on the Church," no. 40.
23. Second Vatican Council, "Decree on Ecumenism," no. 4.

Chapter Four
The Apostolic Church: Leadership and Authority in the Body of Christ

1. Clement of Rome, "Clement's First Letter," 42:4-5, Richardson, p. 62.
2. Henry Chadwick, *The Early Church,* pp. 46-47.
3. The *Didache* (or "The Teaching of the Twelve Apostles"), 15:1-2, in *Early Christian Fathers,* Cyril Richardson, ed., p. 178.
4. See Henry Chadwick, *The Early Church,* p. 51.
5. Ignatius of Antioch, "Letter to the Trallians," 2:1-3, in *Early Christian Fathers,* Cyril Richardson, ed., pp. 98, 99.
6. Ibid., "Letter to the Trallians," 3:1, p. 99.
7. Ignatius of Antioch, "Letter to the Smyrneans," 8:1-2, in *Early Christian Fathers,* p. 115.
8. John de Satge, *Peter and the Single Church* (London: SPCK, 1981), p. 45.
9. Second Vatican Council, "Dogmatic Constitution on the Church," no. 25.

Chapter Five
The Pope: A Chief Witness to Jesus and Sign of the Church's Unity

1. For reliable Catholic and Protestant commentaries that support this interpretation of Matthew 16:18, see the *Jerome Biblical Commentary* (p. 92), *Peake's Commentary* (p. 787), the *Interpreter's Bible* (pp. 450-451), and *Peter in the New Testament,* Raymond Brown, Karl Donfried, John Reumann, eds (Augsburg/Paulist Press, 1973).
2. Cf. Gn 2:19-23, 3:30, 4:1, 5:29, 16:11, 17:5, 32:29, 41:45; 1 Sm 1:20; 2 Kgs 24:17; 2 Chr 36:4; Nm 13:9-17; Is 8:3, 17:14, 62:2; Hos 2:16ff; Dn 1:17.
3. Clement of Rome, "Clement's First Letter," in *Early Christian Fathers,* Cyril Richardson, ed., p. 70.
4. Ignatius of Antioch, "Letter to the Romans," introduction, in *Early Christian Fathers,* Cyril Richardson, ed., p. 103.
5. Irenaeus of Lyons, "Refutation and Overthrow of the Knowledge Falsely So Called" (*Against Heresies*), book III, 3:2, in *Early Christian Fathers,* p. 372.
6. Cyprian of Carthage, "On the Unity of the Catholic Church," 4 in *The*

Faith of the Early Fathers, vol. 1, W.A. Jurgens, ed., pp. 220-21.
7. Ambrose of Milan, "Commentary on the Psalms," 40:30, quoted in *Dogma 4: The Church,* Michael Schmaus (Kansas City: Sheed and Ward, 1972), p. 184.
8. St. Jerome, Letters, 15:2, quoted in *Dogma 4: The Church,* p. 184.
9. Henry Chadwick, *The Early Church,* pp. 237f.
10. Ibid., pp. 238, 240, 241. Also Paolo Brezzi, *The Papacy: Its Origin and Historical Evolution* (Westminster, Md.: Newman, 1958), p. 48.
11. Paolo Brezzi, *The Papacy,* p. 49.
12. Augustine of Hippo, Sermon 131, quoted in Paolo Brezzi, *The Papacy,* p. 55.
13. Thomas Bokenkotter, *A Concise History of the Catholic Church* (Garden City, N.Y.: Doubleday, 1979), p. 98. Also see Chadwick, *The Early Church,* p. 243, and Schmaus, *Dogma 4: The Church,* p. 188.
14. Ibid., pp. 110-12. Paolo Brezzi, *The Papacy,* pp. 69-74; *Dogma 4: The Church,* p. 188.
15. First Vatican Council, *Pastor Aeternus,* chap. 3, in *Documents of Vatican I,* John F. Broderick, S.J., trans. (Collegeville, Minn.: Liturgical Press, 1971), p. 58. The quote from Pope Gregory I is from his Letter to Eulogius of Alexandria, in *Epistolae,* Bk 8, n. 29 (30 in some editions).
16. Augustine of Hippo, Sermon 340, no. 1.
17. First Vatican Council, *Pastor Aeternus,* chap. 4, in *Documents of Vatican I,* p. 63.
18. Second Vatican Council, "Dogmatic Constitution on the Church," no. 25.
19. Second Vatican Council, "Dogmatic Constitution on the Church," no. 25.

Chapter Six
The Holy Spirit

1. Second Vatican Council, "Dogmatic Constitution on the Church," no. 4.
2. Pope John XXIII, *Humanae Salutis,* Dec. 25, 1961, quoted in *The Documents of Vatican II,* Walter Abbott, ed., p. 709.
3. See "Pope Paul Addresses the Charismatic Renewal," *New Covenant,* July 1975, pp. 23-26, and Pope John Paul II, "The Church Has Seen the Fruits of Your Devotion," *New Covenant,* August, 1981, pp. 7-9.
4. Francis Sullivan, S.J., *Charisms and Charismatic Renewal: A Biblical and Theological Study* (Ann Arbor, Mich.: Servant Books, 1982), pp. 70-71.
5. *Summa Theologiae* I, q. 43, a.6, quoted in *Charisms and Charismatic Renewal,* p. 71.
6. *Charisms and Charismatic Renewal,* pp. 71-72.
7. Ibid., p. 72.
8. Ibid., p. 74.
9. Second Vatican Council, "Dogmatic Constitution on the Church," no. 12.
10. Ibid.

11. Second Vatican Council, "Decree on the Apostolate of the Laity," no. 3.
12. Ibid.

Chapter Seven
The Sacraments

1. Second Vatican Council, "Dogmatic Constitution on the Church," no. 1.
2. Ibid., no. 48.
3. Second Vatican Council, "Constitution on the Sacred Liturgy," no. 7.
4. Ibid.
5. Ignatius of Antioch, "Letter to the Smyrneans, 8:2, in *Early Christian Fathers,* Cyril Richardson, ed., p. 115.
6. This understanding of the Eucharist is presented in a number of official and unoffical sources of Catholic teaching. The Council of Trent said that in the Eucharist . . . "the victory and triumph of his death are again made present." A recent Catholic catechism summarizes it well, and also includes another quotation from the Council of Trent:

> Jesus does not die and rise again every time the Eucharistic liturgy is enacted, but his one sacrifice is made present to men in every celebration of Mass. The God-Man instituted the Mass with an ecclesial dimension—its ability to be carried on everywhere in the Church—so that the "bloody sacrifice which was once offered on the cross should be made present, its memory preserved to the end of the world, and its salvation-bringing power applied to the forgiveness of the sins which are daily committed by us." (The Teaching of Christ, p. 426)

The Roman Catholic teaching is officially presented in the Documents of Second Vatican Council:

> At the Last Supper, on the night he was betrayed, our Savior instituted the eucharistic sacrifice of his Body and Blood. This he did in order to *perpetuate* the sacrifice of the Cross through the ages until he should come again, and so entrust to his beloved Spouse, the Church, a memorial of his death and resurrection: a Sacrament of love, a sign of unity, a bond of charity, a paschal banquet in which Christ is consumed, the mind is filled with grace, and a pledge of future glory is given to us. (Constitution on the Sacred Liturgy, 47).

To "perpetuate" something does not mean to repeat it. "Perpetuate" means "to make perpetual or to cause to last indefinitely." "Perpetual" means either "continuing forever" or "valid for all time." The point is that Roman Catholics do not believe that Jesus is sacrificed again at each Mass, but that the *one,* eternal, "continuing forever," "valid for all time" sacrifice of Jesus Christ on Calvary is enacted and made present to those who participate.

Another common misunderstanding of Catholic belief about the Mass and the Eucharist is the Catholic practice of "offering a Mass" for someone, or saying Mass "in honor of" a saint or holy person. This is explained well by a recent Catholic cathechism:

> A mass may be offered on the occasion of a saint's feast, and give incidental honor to the saint. But the sacrifice of Christ is offered only to God, for He alone is worthy of this perfect adoration and praise. Masses may be offered for the needs of an individual person, living or deceased, but no Mass can be offered exclusively for such a limited intention. Every Mass is offered chiefly by Christ, and His ministerial priest must share His universal saving purposes. The Mass is offered to glorify God, to bring salvation to all, to make present and accessible the limitless riches of Christ. (*The Teaching of Christ*, p. 427).

7. Second Vatican Council, "Dogmatic Constitution on the Church," no. 10.
8. Second Vatican Council, "Constitution on the Sacred Liturgy," no. 10.
9. Ibid., no. 9 and 11.
10. Some Christians object to the distinction between "serious (or mortal) sin" and "less serious (or venial) sins." Many would say that all sin is serious. However, the Bible makes this distinction between mortal or deadly sin and sin that is not deadly in 1 Jn 5:16-17.
11. Here I will briefly review in more detail how the forgiveness of serious sin was administered by the elders of the Christian church. The only evidence in the second century was in "The Shepherd" of Hermas, in which Hermas speaks of a second "penance" after baptism, instituted by the Lord and entrusted to the Shepherd, a term that seems to refer to the bishop as pastor of his flock, (New Catholic Enyclopedia, XI, p. 74). From the third to the fifth century, harsh public penances were imposed by the bishops in case of serious sin. Penance was allowed only once after baptism, because a baptized Christian was believed to be freed from serious sin and was expected to live the fullness of love received in baptism. Penance was called by St. Gregory of Nazianzus and St. John Damascene a "second and more laborious baptism."

The story of the practice of public penance during this period is fascinating, and reflects how heinous serious sin was considered by the early church. The lengths of public penances ranged from three to twenty-five years, depending on the seriousness of the sin and the office of the offender in the church. (Bishops, priests, and deacons were judged more harshly.) During the time of the penance, the penitent was excluded from celebrating or receiving the Eucharist with the rest of the Christian community. When the penance was completed, the person was received back into full communion through a ceremony of reconciliation with the church led by the bishop (or an appointed representative).

Up through the fifth century, all records show that the forgiveness of serious sin was done through public confession, penance, and reconciliation, and was administered by the bishop or his designated representative. Private confession and penance began among the Irish and Celtic churches during the sixth and seventh centuries. Apparently due to their distance from continental Europe, they were not familiar with public confession. The religious life of these people centered around abbeys. There were priest-monks, who heard confessions, administered penance, and reconciled the penitents in private fashion, similar to the current practice in the Roman Catholic Church. However, the penances were still severe, and the penitent could not be reconciled until the completion of the penance. Forgiveness for serious sin could also be given more than once, which was not the practice on the Continent. The practice of private confession and penance eventually spread to the Continent and gradually was accepted in place of public confession. Once again, only priests and bishops were recognized as having this authority to forgive sins in God's name.

After one or two further developments, penance appeared in a form very similar to the way it is practiced today in the Roman Catholic Church. In the eleventh century, it became common for sins to be absolved (forgiven) at the time of confession, rather than after the penance was completed. In 1215 A.D., the Fourth Lateran Council obligated all Christians to confess their sins at least once a year, if they were in serious sin, especially in preparation to receive the Eucharist at Easter. This is still the practice of the Catholic Church today. By the fourteenth century, public penances had become rare and had virtually disappeared by the sixteenth. Also in the sixteenth century, penance was formally declared a sacrament of the Catholic Church by the Council of Trent. Although it had been practiced and viewed as a sacrament throughout the history of Christianity, it was necessary to formally define it as such in response to the Protestant reformers, who questioned or rejected penance as a sacrament or the way it was administered by the priests of the Catholic Church.

12. Second Vatican Council, "Decree on the Bishops' Pastoral Office in the Church," no. 15.

Chapter Eight
The Communion of Saints

1. Second Vatican Council, "Dogmatic Constitution on the Church," no. 49.
2. Ibid.
3. C.S. Lewis, *The Screwtape Letters* (New York: Macmillan, 1961), p. 12.
4. The Bible does warn about leaving judgment to the Lord, but Catholic Christians have always taken this to mean avoiding *negative* judgment on anyone's salvation. The Catholic Church declares many people to be

"saints" to enable us to imitate them and ask for their prayers, but it has never declared that anyone is assuredly damned.

5. Second Vatican Council, "Dogmatic Constitution on the Church," no. 50.
6. St. Jerome, Letter against Vigilantius (406 A.D.), in *The Faith of the Early Fathers,* vol. 2, W.A. Jurgens, trans., p. 206.
7. Augustine of Hippo, "Against Faustus the Manichaean" (c. 400 A.D.), 20, 21, in *The Faith of the Early Fathers,* vol. 3, W.A. Jurgens, trans., p. 59.
8. Tertullian, "The Crown," 3, 2, in *The Faith of the Early Fathers,* vol. 1, W.A. Jurgens, ed., p. 151.
9. Augustine of Hippo, *The City of God,* book XX, 9, 2 in *The Faith of the Early Fathers,* vol. 3, W.A. Jurgens, ed., p. 104.
10. Second Vatican Council, "Dogmatic Constitution on the Church," no. 50.

Chapter Nine
Mary

1. Second Vatican Council, "Dogmatic Constitution on the Church," no. 67.
2. Fr. Kilian McDonnell, O.S.B., "Protestants, Pentecostals, and Mary," *New Covenant,* March 1977, pp. 28-29.
3. Justin Martyr (d. 165) was the first theologian of salvation history who contrasted Mary, "the Mother of the Redeemer" with Eve, "the Mother of sin and death" (Dialogue with Trypho, c. 150).
4. Irenaeus of Lyons, "On the Refutation and Overthrow of Knowledge Falsely So Called" or "Against Heresies," book III, 22, 4, in *The Faith of the Early Fathers,* vol. 1, W.A. Jurgens, ed., p. 93.
5. Kilian McDonnell explains this more fully in his article, "Protestants, Pentecostals, and Mary," *New Covenant,* March 1977, p. 28:

The ark, which was placed in a tent, or tabernacle, was like a portable temple. It was probably a rectangular box about the size of an ordinary trunk and had poles attached so that men could carry it on their shoulders. The Israelites considered it Yahweh's throne, the place in which he manifested his presence. From between the two angels on the ark God spoke to Moses (Ex 25:22). It was an object of veneration among the Israelites, and they even carried it into battle so that the Presence would be with them (1 Sm 4:3-11).

Luke uses the ark and the Presence as depicted in the book of Exodus to explain the function of Mary. The presence of Yahweh over the ark of the covenant is the model for explaining the Presence of the Most High over Mary. The consequences of this manifestation of the Presence are similar: the ark "is filled with the Glory," and Mary is filled with the presence of "the Holy One," and "Son of God."

The cloud of the Presence covered the ark from the outside, and the glory of God filled its interior. So also the Holy Spirit descends upon

Mary, the "woman-ark." She is overshadowed by the Holy Spirit and filled with the Presence. Like the ark, she becomes the dwelling place of God.

When Luke writes of Mary's visit to Elizabeth (1:39-45), he again uses the model of the ark in a subtle way. There is an interesting parallel between this Lucan text and 2 Samuel 6:2-19. In Samuel we see the joy of the people of Jerusalem when David brings the ark into the city. In Luke, we encounter the joy of Elizabeth and of her infant at the visit of Mary who carries within her the Presence. Compare the dance of David before the ark in the book of Samuel and the leap of John the Baptist in his mother's womb in the gospel of Luke.

The ark and Mary have this in common: they are filled with the Presence and they carry it with them. They are not themselves the Presence but they have a unique function in its regard.

6. The Second Vatican Council explained the concept in the "Dogmatic Constitution on the Church," no. 62 and 63.
7. Second Vatican Council, "Dogmatic Constitution on the Church," no. 60.
8. Ibid., no. 62.
9. See "The Virginity of Mary," in *Theotokos: A Theological Encyclopedia of the Blessed Virgin Mary,* Michael O'Carroll, C.S.Sp., (Wilmington, Del.: Michael Glazier, Inc., 1982), pp. 357-61.
10. Raymond Brown, Karl Donfried, Joseph Fitzmeyer, John Reumann, eds., *Mary in the New Testament* (New York: Paulist, 1978), pp. 65-67, 291.
11. Ibid.
12. Council of Ephesus (431 A.D.), "The Anathemas of the Chapter of Cyril against Nestorius," canon 1, in *The Sources of Catholic Doctrine* (Denzinger), trans. Roy Defferari (St. Louis, Mo.: Bitterden Books, 1957), p. 50.
13. *Jesus Christ, Centre of the Christian Life,* Canadian Conference of Catholic Bishops, Ottawa: Publication Service of CCCB, 1981, p. 23.
14. Ambrose of Milan, "Commentary on Psalm 118," 22, 30, in *Faith of the Early Fathers,* vol. 2, W.A. Jurgens, ed., p. 166.
15. Augustine of Hippo, "Nature and Grace," 36, 42, in *The Faith of the Early Fathers,* vol. 3, p. 111.
16. Fr. Edward O'Connor, C.S.C., "The Development of Marian Doctrine in the Church," *God's Word Today,* May 1982, pp. 93-94.
17. Fr. Raymond Brown, S.S., "Mary in the New Testament and in Catholic Life," *America,* May 15, 1982, p. 378.
18. Pope Pius IX, "Ineffabilis Deus," Dec. 8, 1854, quoted in *The Sources of Catholic Dogma,* p. 413.
19. Frances Parkinson Keyes, "Bernadette and the Beautiful Lady," in *A Woman Clothed with the Sun,* John Delaney, ed. (Garden City, N.Y.: Doubleday Image Books, 1960), p. 137.
20. Pope Pius XIII, "Munificentissimus Deus," quoted in *Theotokos: A*

Theological Encyclopedia of the Blessed Virgin Mary, p. 55.
21. See "The Assumption of Our Lady" in *Theotokos: A Theological Encyclopedia of the Blessed Virgin Mary,* pp. 55-57.
22. Pope Paul VI, "Devotion to the Blessed Virgin Mary," no. 55 (*Marialis Cultus*), Feb. 2, 1974 (Washington, D.C.: United States Catholic Conference, 1974), p. 37.
23. Pope John Paul II, homily at Fatima, Portugal, May 13, 1982.
24. Fr. John Bertolucci, unpublished address at the Franciscan University of Steubenvile, Ohio, Spring, 1983.
25. Ethel Cook Eliot, "Our Lady of Guadalupe in Mexico," in *A Woman Clothed with the Sun,* pp. 39-60.
26. William C. McGrath, "Our Lady of the Rosary," in *A Woman Clothed with the Sun,* pp. 175-212.
27. Ibid., pp. 202-203.
28. Fr. Francis Martin, unpublished address at the Franciscan University of Steubenville, Ohio, Fall, 1982.

Chapter Ten
Man's Destiny in Christ

1. Tertullian, "The Crown" (A.D. 211), 3, 2, in *The Faith of the Early Fathers,* p. 151.
2. George Maloney, *The Everlasting Now* (Notre Dame, Ind.: Ave Maria, 1980) pp. 64-65.
3. Second Vatican Council, "Dogmatic Constitution on the Church," no. 50.
4. See James Manney, "Heaven on Earth: Rapture, Tribulation, and Millennialism," *God's Word Today,* December 1982, pp. 47-48.

Index

and "baptism in the Spirit," 106-
108
circumcision parallel to, 126
commission to perform, 124
confirmation and, 140-41
delay of, 139
effects of, 125
and the Eucharist, 137
importance for salvation, 27-28,
39, 124
of infants, 126-29, 141
Jesus on, 28
and membership in the church,
29-30
Paul on, 28, 101-102
and re-baptism, 128-29
and reception of the Spirit, 101-
102, 103, 124-25, 140
renewal of, 23
by water, 102, 105, 125
"Baptism in the Spirit":
alternate terms for, 106
Catholic theology and, 106-109
confirmation and, 105, 107-108,
141
experience of, 106-107, 109-111
meaning of, 104-106
prayer for, 108-109, 110
Basil, St., 198
Beatific vision, 192 (*see also* Heaven)
Bertolucci, Fr. John, 185
Bible:
authority of, 49-50
canon of, 49
development of, 42-49
on faith and good works, 24-25
on free will, 21
on hope in salvation, 32-33
inerrancy of, 41
on infant baptism, 126-27
inspiration of, 6, 49-50
on intercession of the saints, 157
interpretation of, 50-53, 81,
173-74
on Mary, 167
as a norm of belief, 6

and papal teaching office, 98
the primary work of revelation, 7,
41, 47
a product of the church, 42-43
and purgatory, 223
and religious expression, 51-52
and the second coming of Christ,
226
significance of name-giving in,
86-87
and tradition, 42, 47-50, 52-53
Bishops:
apostolic succession and, 30-31,
45-47, 72-73, 88-89, 133, 138
authority of, 30-31, 46, 52, 74-
81, 135, 138
celibacy of, 74
charismatic gifts and, 115, 117
as church elders, 45-46
councils of, 79-80
and the development of the Bible,
47-50
discernment of tradition, 50, 52-
53, 173-74
duties of, 45, 47, 50, 74-78, 117
duty to teach and interpret the
word of God, 31, 45, 50
forgiveness of sins by, 138
infallibility of, 51, 80-81, 94
leadership of the Mass, 77, 133,
135
local, 76-78
relationship to the pope, 93
represents Jesus Christ, 76, 78
submission to biblical authority,
50, 53
teaching office of, 45-46, 49-50,
74-76
title of, 74
Body of Christ (*see* Church)
"Born-again" Catholics, 102-103
Brown, Raymond, S.S., 178

Calvin, John, 174
Canonization, process of, 155
Canon law, code of, 134

and the indwelling of the holy
Spirit, 111-12
of the saints, 154-55, 156
and sin, 66-67
Holy Orders, sacrament of, 143-48
(*see also* Priests/presbyters,
Priesthood)
celibacy and, 144-46
"laying on of hands" and, 143-44
and the ordination of women, 147
origin of, 143-44
and priestly qualities, 147-48
Holy Spirit: (*see also* "Baptism in the
Spirit," Charismatic gifts of the
Spirit, Gifts of the Holy Spirit):
Aquinas on, 107-108
and authority, 31, 138
baptism and, 27, 101-103, 125
and the charismatic movement,
99
and the Christian religion, 7
confirmation and, 140-43
and the development of the Bible,
42-43
experience of, 104, 106-107, 110-
11
and forgiveness of sin, 73, 138
fruit of, 103 104, 111
gifts of, 111-14
as God's gift to each Christian,
101-103, 105-106
guides the church, 31, 42, 51, 79,
100,
and hierarchy of truths, 10, 11, 12
indwelling of, 100, 107-108,
109-110, 170
infallibility and, 79-80, 94-95
Jesus and, 101, 111
and Mary, 167-68
and the meaning of Christianity,
99-101
and the papacy, 87-88
reveals God's truth, 7, 100
sanctifies the church, 100, 113,
116

signs of the presence of, 111-12,
114
and work among Christians, 99-
117
Hope:
the call to, 8
the final revelation of Christ and,
203
loss of, 33
perseverance in, 34-38
in salvation, 32-33, 37-38, 39,
204

Ignatius of Antioch:
on the catholicity of the church,
58
on the church at Rome, 89
on deacons, 77
on episcopal authority, 46, 77,
133
on leadership of the Eucharist,
133
on presbyters, 77
Immaculate Conception, doctrine
of (*see also* Mary), 201-205
definition of, 96, 179
doctrine of the Assumption and,
180
does not contradict Scripture,
179
difficulty of belief in, 173
Jesus and, 177
Lourdes and, 179
Mary's need for redemption and,
176-77
objections to, 177-78
Incarnation:
and God's relationship to mankind, 7-8
implication of, 8-9
Jesus and, 16-17
principle of, 7-9, 117, 120-22,
139, 156, 159
Infallibility:
of bishops, 50-51, 79-81

private, 6, 184-85
public, 50
sources of, 7
through the Holy Spirit, 6-7
transmission of, 52-53, 184
Revelation, Book of:
  on heaven, 192
  on the millenium, 199
  on perseverance in faith, 37
Rome, bishop of (*see* Pope)
Rome, church of
  (*see also* Catholic Church):
  and the "apostolic see," 91
  canon of the New Testament
    developed by, 49
  and other local churches, 89
  preeminence of, 46-47, 52, 88
  and Western Christianity, 61
Rosary, the, 182-84
  as a Christian prayer, 183-84
  as a meditation, 183
  "mysteries" of, 183
  prayers contained in, 183

Sacramentals, 8, 160
Sacraments:
  and "baptism in the Holy Spirit,"
    106-108
  effective visible signs, 8, 122-23
  established by Jesus, 121, 122-23
  incarnational principle and, 120-
    22
  Jesus as the primary, 120-21, 150
  meaningless without faith, 24,
    150
  as a means of grace, 23, 27, 108,
    119-20, 150
  number of, 123
  power of, 119-20
  and salvation, 27-28, 103
  term for, 123
Saints
  (*see also* Communion of
    saints):
  canonization of, 155
  communion of, 151-62

definition of, 151-52
existence of in heaven, 152-53
and the "full gospel," 10-11
holiness of, 154
honor given to, 158, 161-62
images and relics of, 159-60
and the incarnational principle,
  155-56
intercession of, 157-58
as models, 155-56
recognized by Catholic Church,
  34-35, 154-55
Salvation, 13-39
acceptance of, 21-24, 27, 32, 39
accomplished by Jesus, 16, 192
applied to Mary, 176-77, 180
church law and, 30-32
cosmic dimensions of, 16
Council of Trent on, 25-26
and eternal life, 17-18
a gift, not earned, 17, 128
and hope, 32-38
importance of church for, 28-30
knowledge of, 32-38
meaning of for Catholics, 17-39
and missionary activity, 18-19
necessity to preach, 20
of non-believers, 20
only through Jesus, 17-20, 181
outside the church, 29
possibility of the loss of, 31, 33,
  36
presumption concerning, 33
primacy of faith in obtaining, 24
as a process, 24, 38-39, 103
proclamation of, 19
revealed in the Old Testament, 15
role of the sacraments in, 27-28
Trinity and, 13-14
universality of, 192
Satan:
  and the communion of saints, 154
  deceived mankind, 15
  end of time and, 199
  overcome by Jesus, 16
  and the prophecy of salvation, 15